GOOD NEIGHBOR CAMPAIGN
HANDBOOK

Good Neighbor Campaign Handbook

How to Win

Contributors

Rachael Belz
Hilton Kelley
Kim Klein
Denny Larson
Teresa Mills
John O'Connor
Paul Ryder

Foreword by Sandy Buchanan
Edited by Paul Ryder

iUniverse, Inc.
New York Lincoln Shanghai

Good Neighbor Campaign Handbook
HOW TO WIN

iUniverse books may be ordered through booksellers or by contacting:

iUniverse
2021 Pine Lake Road, Suite 100
Lincoln, NE 68512
www.iuniverse.com
1-800-Authors (1-800-288-4677)

Cover photo: Laura Rench, Michelle Cooper, Jane Forrest Redfern and Mary Johnson celebrate after a united community campaign forced the U.S. Army to abandon its plan to treat VX nerve agent hydrolysate in Dayton, October 14, 2003. Reproduced by permission of photographer Jan Underwood and the *Dayton Daily News*.

ISBN-13: 978-0-595-38651-2 (pbk)
ISBN-13: 978-0-595-83032-9 (ebk)
ISBN-10: 0-595-38651-2 (pbk)
ISBN-10: 0-595-83032-3 (ebk)

Printed in the United States of America

To John O'Connor
1954–2001

CONTENTS

▼

Foreword

This handbook is dedicated to the memory of John O'Connor, founder of the National Toxics Campaign. John's life was cut short by a heart attack when he was only 46 years old. In the time he had on earth, he left behind a legacy that people twice his age would envy. John was a thinker, a writer, a philanthropist, a mentor, a true friend, a Red Sox fan, a basketball fanatic, even at one time a candidate for Congress. Above all, though, he was an organizer.

John understood that the fundamentals of community organizing never change. In fact, he was such a good teacher that we were able to excerpt his chapter on "Organizing to Win" in this book without changing a word, even though it was written fifteen years ago for the manual *Fighting Toxics*, edited by John and Gary Cohen.

John's passion for preventing toxic chemical exposures originated with the baseball diamond he played on as a child in Massachusetts, which was later found to be an asbestos dump. As an adult, he worked with community groups around the country who wanted to clean up hazardous waste dumps or get a local industry to change its practices to prevent pollution.

The passage of the national toxic chemical right-to-know law, as part of the Superfund law in 1986, was a direct result of the work of the National Toxics Campaign. Leading up to the Congressional vote, the campaign organized the "Superdrive for Superfund," where four trucks started at different parts of the country and visited communities all around the nation on their way to Washington, D.C. We all have many wild and wonderful memories from those days, especially of John cranking up Bruce Springs-teen's *Born in the USA* full blast as he'd drive the rickety Superdrive truck, filled with toxic waste samples, picket signs, and petitions, and pull into a town to load up with more evidence to take to Congress.

John worked on many community organizing campaigns in the Boston area over the years, but in 2001 returned to Ohio to do two training ses-sions for Ohio Citizen Action's "good neighbor campaigns." He trained a new generation of neighborhood and canvass activists on how to exercise the three rights he always emphasized: the right to know, the right to inspect, and the right to negotiate.

A third trip to Ohio in 2001 was typical of John's generous nature. In April, our dear friend Ed Kelly died of cancer in Boston. Ed and John worked together on all kinds of issues in Boston from electric deregulation to the Irish Famine Memorial. Ed was also one of the founders of Ohio Citizen Action, and had many close friends in Ohio from his years in Cleveland. John organized a group of Ed's friends and family to come to Cleveland in August for a Red Sox/Indians game and get-together to cele-brate Ed's life. Of course, none of us knew then that we would lose John a few months later.

But, in a way, John will always be with us: a voice in our ear, egging us on to knock on one more door, to get just one more person involved, to try just one more campaign idea. I think he'd like this book.

Sandy Buchanan
Executive Director
Ohio Citizen Action

Acknowledgements

Thanks are first due to the thousands of good neighbors around the country whose campaigns produced the lessons assembled here.

Thanks also to the contributors and to Angela Oster and Aaron Koonce for the illustrations. The following people helped prepare the text: David Altman, Mary Carmen Cupito, Brian Dunn, Stephen Gabor, Stu Greenberg, Ellis Jacobs, Christine Knapp, Jessica Kramer, Jennifer O'Donnell, Sara O'Neal, Anne Rolfes, Joanne Rossi, Tom Stevick, Rich Swirsky, Michelle Taphorn, Simona Vaclavikova, Noreen Warnock, and Jeanne Zokovitch.

This handbook is a project of Ohio Citizen Action and the Ohio Citizen Action Education Fund. The organizations are stronger than ever in their 31st year, largely due to the relentless work of the two boards and senior staff, led by Ohio Citizen Action Board President Ellis Jacobs, Ohio Citizen Action Education Fund Board President Bruce French, Ohio Citizen Action Executive Director Sandy Buchanan and Ohio Citizen Action Education Fund Executive Director Rachael Belz.

The boards of directors include Rhonda Barnes-Kloth, Caroline Beidler, Sandy Bihn, Jennifer Cooper, Lisa Crawford, Melissa English, Dr. Kathy Fagan, Kim Foreman, Mary Johnson, Mike Jones, Joe Korff, Marie Kocoshis, Hal Madorsky, Rick Topper, and Tom Trimble.

The senior staff includes Alison Baker, Ruth Breech, Sarah Corbin, Crystal Cottrill, Sara Dalton, Jason Danklefson, Christa Ebert, Stephen Gabor, Shelley Gross, Sarah Grutza, Brandon Milne, Curt Moultine,

Angela Oster, Lynn Scheerhorn, Michelle Taphorn, Catherine Turcer, Simona Vaclavikova, Don Wolcott, Tim Wrightsman and Chris Young.

We remember fondly our board member Art Minson, who died in December 2005 at the age of 91. With his lifelong commitment to his community in East Akron, Art was the best kind of neighbor anyone could have.

Thanks to the George Gund Foundation for its generous financial support.

Preface

This handbook is for neighbors of polluting companies who are considering launching a good neighbor campaign, or who find themselves in the middle of one.

Such campaigns are the alternative to waiting around for the government to do something. Stringent laws and stringent enforcement remain a fantasy. Stringent neighbors are not a fantasy. We can get the job done ourselves.

While we offer no guarantees, every tactic and approach in the handbook has worked in at least one campaign, and most have worked many times. We think you will find these ideas fit together in a way that makes them remarkably powerful.

The book assumes the company is already in the neighborhood and both the company and the neighbors want it to stay. Many of the lessons can be helpful in other circumstances as well, however, such as where a company cannot coexist with the neighbors (a "good-bye neighbor campaign"); where a company has fled, leaving a contaminated site; or where a company wants to site a new facility in the neighborhood.

A few people have cautioned us not to give away too much "that our opponents could learn from." What if this handbook should fall into the wrong hands? On the contrary, we believe the "right hands" include those attached to corporate CEOs and plant managers. As you will read, the more companies understand about these campaigns, the more likely a good outcome for everyone.

One of our favorite good neighbor campaigns was also our briefest. In February 1989, a train derailed near some B.F. Goodrich toxic chemical storage tanks in Akron, Ohio. When the train overturned and caught fire, thousands of neighbors had to evacuate. Ohio Citizen Action, local PTAs, and neighbor groups started meeting with Goodrich officials about waste reduction. Ohio Citizen Action's Richard Swirsky told Goodrich officials we were preparing a report that would rank B.F. Goodrich as the worst air toxics polluter in the county. Goodrich decided to "get ahead of the issue." The day the report came out, Goodrich executives announced a plan to cut toxic air emissions by 70% over three years. In the end, the company cut emissions by more than 90%.

Smart company, short campaign.

CHAPTER 1

▼

"WHY WOULD YOU WANT TO BUILD A COMMUNITY CENTER IN SUCH A POLLUTED COMMUNITY?"

Hilton Kelley

In 1901, oil erupted from a derrick on Spindletop Hill near the Texas-Lou-isiana border. Within three months, six wells on the hill were out-producing the rest of the world combined. In the century since, refineries and chemical plants have settled like crows from Corpus Christi to New Orleans. Port Arthur, Texas has more than its share: Huntsman, Motiva, Premcor, BASF, Atofina, and Chevron Phillips.

In 2000, Hilton Kelley, a son of Port Arthur, had made his way to Holly-wood for a career as an actor and stuntman. His plans changed. "I was work-ing on the television show 'Nash Bridges' with Don Johnson. I decided to make a visit home, like I did every few years, and what I found was beyond belief. Because of the increasing air pollution, the people of Port Arthur were too sick to help themselves. They were beat down. The town was dying, and I saw a need that I thought I could fill."[1] Three months later, Kelley moved back home.

Kelley is now Executive Director of Port Arthur's Community In-power and Development Association, Field Coordinator of the National Refinery Reform Campaign and Chair of the National Bucket Brigade Coalition.—Ed.

Coming home to Port Arthur

All my life, I've been doing something in my community. I was raised that way. I was a Boy Scout. I hate to see litter on the street. I hate to see people defacing property. We're supposed to keep our community clean and beautiful.

When I was a kid coming up, I would work with kids like myself, getting them off the street and into structured organizations like Scouting. I believed in that lifestyle, getting people to move in the right direction. I had a burning desire to pitch in and help out no matter where I was.

When I was in Oakland, I ran into a guy who worked at the Lockwood Gardens housing project. He knew I was into acting, and he asked me to come and talk to the kids the next day. I spoke with the kids about following their dreams. "You can make it if you try." "Put your best foot forward." They invited me to come back, and we started talking about putting together an after school program.

The kids sat down and wrote about what went on in their everyday lives, what they saw every day in the housing projects, and how they felt about it. After I read their papers, I asked them to write a play about how they would handle those situations. It gave them an opportunity to look at their situation, police their situation in their own minds, and see for themselves that they could make things better. They came up with their own solutions. We wrote little scripts and they got up on stage and rehearsed them. We invited their parents to come see this 30-minute skit. Then we had a talent show. Some of the kids could sing, some could dance, and some could do art. It was fun and it motivated their spirit.

---

1. Donovan Webster, Michael Scherer, "No Clear Skies," *Mother Jones* magazine, September-October, 2003.

In 2000, I had a premonition that I had to go back to Port Arthur. It was really a godsend. I'm a Baptist myself and I believe in God. That's who gets me through the day. Without Him, nothing is possible, and with Him, all things are possible. When I was given this premonition, I packed up everything in Oakland and put the acting thing on hold for a while. I moved back to Port Arthur to do exactly what I'm doing now, helping people who needed someone to step up to the plate and be responsible.

There were no community centers in our community in Port Arthur. When I came back home, I was interested in starting one to help give kids guidance in life. Kids were hanging out and getting in trouble. The government was building more prisons but no recreation for kids. In my opinion, they were setting the young people up to be incarcerated.

I was born in 1960. As long as I can remember our community smelled like rotten eggs because of the sulfur from the refineries. At nighttime, we had a bright orange sky because the refineries were constantly flaring, burning off fumes and gas. I never gave it any thought because it was just part of life.

Rev. Alfred Dominic, a lifelong Port Arthur resident, put a question to me. He asked, "Why would you want to build a community center in such a polluted community?"

Understanding what's wrong

We started to do a little research and a whole new world opened up. We found laws on the books to protect citizens from these dangerous gases we'd been breathing. We found a state regulatory agency that keeps files on refineries when they have "emission events" and upsets. We started to go through plant records and found out that not only were upsets and flarings their way of doing business, but they were also illegal.[2] The EPA has a

---

2. For a while, Erin Koenig at the *Beaumont Examiner* reported every upset in the Port Arthur area. She would report the chemicals being released, how much, what company did it, and what they would do to the human body. She should have been commended, but instead she was released. She was a good friend to the environmental community in our area. We hold her in high regard.

limit on how long a facility can flare, and these guys had been in violation for years. The federal government was not enforcing the clean air laws and the state regulatory agency was not issuing violations either. No one was doing anything.

I heard from the mouths of refinery engineers that many times they had prayed that the stuff they released would get up high enough until it dissipated. Many of these guys had information that, if they would have come forward publicly, could have made these industries spend millions of dollars changing their whole plant around. I asked them, "How could you not give that information to the media? You and your whole family live in this community." They told me they were afraid of losing their jobs, the bread on the table. They were afraid of having to go to work at McDonald's. So instead, they told me this stuff in secret.

I learned that in this town, 35–40% of the people had somebody in their family who died from cancer. Many women aged 14 to 50 discovered fibroid tumors in their uteruses. They can forget about having kids; they are never going to have a child. One little girl fought multiple brain tumors for two years, while her mother brought her back and forth from the M.D. Anderson Cancer Center in Houston. She finally succumbed to the disease and died at sixteen years old. Her whole life was ahead of her.

People throughout the community had skin diseases, with little dark spots all over their arms, back and chest. I had it when I was a kid growing up there, but when I moved to California, everything cleared up. When I left Port Arthur, my constant cough stopped. I've been back in Port Arthur for five years now; eventually I'm going to have to take another break from here.

There is definitely something in the air that gets into your blood stream, and is dispersed throughout your body. Your body is constantly trying to fight it off. I believe that over a long time, the body sort of gives up. This is when cancer starts to set in and develop. This is my personal theory.

I knew I had to do something. There comes a time in any man's life when you have to pick a side, whether you want to or not. If you sit neutral, you're not doing a damn thing. You've already picked a side. You're helping the enemy.

Getting started

The way to start is to just get started. Start with you. I was by myself. I got a sign and stood on the corner with it. That's a start. I had my facts, stacked up and ready to hand out to people as they came to the corner and stopped. I handed them a piece of paper. That's a start. I knew somebody would stand with me eventually. Then two more people would come, then three, and then four. And I kept on and kept on. It grew.

I set up a first meeting. Initially there were only two people at my meetings: me and the guy who opened the door to let me in, waiting for me to go home.

Eventually I made a connection. Here's how it happens: You may not speak to your next-door neighbor all the time. When you do, you may never really talk about your problems and they don't talk about their problems. They may have a child suffering from the same illness your child suffers from. Maybe the neighbor down the street has a child with the same problem.

That connection had not been made in Port Arthur until I went door-to-door. I was passing out meeting fliers, talking to people one-on-one, every day. I wore a hole in my shoes.

At one house, I said that the chemicals being released could trigger asthma.

"Oh, my baby has asthma. I can show you right now. See, she has to use this here thing to breathe."

"What is that?" I made a note of that.

[Next door: Knock, knock, knock]

"Yes, ma'am. I'm here with the Community In-power and Development Association. We're going to be holding a meeting pertaining to the chemicals that are being released into the environment. I'd like to speak to you a little bit more about it in detail if I may."

"Yes, come on in. My baby's been having asthma for a long time."

As I went through the neighborhood, I found that one out of every five households had a child with asthma. When I made that connection, more people started coming to the meetings. I told them we were going to start pushing for free medication from these industries that caused the problem. You should not have to pay out of your pocket $150 a pop for pills or the nebulizer and albuterol. It is not your fault that your child is sick.

Community In-power and Development Association

We formed the Community In-power and Development Association, Inc. We have 116 members, of whom 25 are active members who get out there and pound the pavement. Whenever I call a meeting and I really need more people, I can knock on some doors and get as much help as I need. The dues are a dollar, but most of the time that's waived.

Many grassroots people do not have a lot of time for campaigning. They are busy working one or two mediocre jobs paying $5 an hour. It is hard to knock on doors when you are tired from those jobs. They have kids to feed and pick up from school. They are busy worrying about how they are going to pay their bills. Many people in our area are sitting in their homes right now with no light or water because they can't pay their utility bills.

Initially, the Development Association tried to negotiate with the industries. Once, Congressman Nick Lampson arranged a meeting between our group and Premcor. The plant manager, Don Kuenzli, said he didn't want to come to a community meeting where people were going to be "acting like a bunch of monkeys." This is an African-American community. Congressman Lampson had to stand up and say that was uncalled for. That's the arrogance these guys have developed over the years because they've gotten away with whatever they want to.

We brought pollution data to City Hall and showed it to our mayor and city council. Our mayor said it was the price we had to pay. I do not feel that a town the size of Port Arthur, with 57,725 people, should have to pay the price for the whole nation to have gasoline. That burden should be shared.

In November 2004, we had a march from the government housing project all the way to City Hall to face off with our city officials. We went up in their offices and urged them to come outside and talk to the people about pollution. They were reluctant, but the city manager came out and then the mayor came out. Then the mayor decided that he didn't want to say anything because people kept asking him questions he could not answer. He went back upstairs. The city manager said he was not equipped to handle pollution questions, "…so don't ask any of those, but any other questions you might want to ask, I can do that."

What really got our members motivated was when they heard the word "lawsuit." We were preparing to sue industry for negligence and unfair treatment. People said, "I want to get involved with that." More people started to come to the meetings. In poor communities, you have to give people something that's tangible. You have to give them some ray of hope that their situation is going to get better. Then you have to make good on it.

Before the Community In-power and Development Association started, the companies had no plan to deal with residents' pollution complaints. Then, about two years ago, they put together a community response team to try to keep neighbors from complaining to the state regulatory agency. They came around to residents and said, "Here's an ink pen and a letter opener from our company, and here's a phone number. If you smell anything, let us know first. Don't call the Texas Commission on Environmental Quality. Don't worry about those guys. We'll come out and deal with the problem. It may just be a gas leak in your kitchen line."

How can you smell all those odors outside if it's just a gas leak in your kitchen line? We encouraged neighbors to call the state regulatory agency, not the company.

Peppering the community with money

The churches tend to be neutral because industry peppers the community with money. Industry is a main source of income for many of the churches. Whenever a church is giving a function, they can ask for a few hundred dollars or a thousand dollars. Industry gives just enough to keep you quiet and keep a smile on your face.

Our county gave Motiva Enterprises a tax abatement in January 2005 that will cost the schools $3.6 million a year. In return, Motiva gave each school $1,000. There are only seven schools in the area, so that is $7,000 back. There are always pictures in the news with a little child pointing to a test tube. The refinery guy is standing over him with a smile like he sponsored this whole project. It cost them all of $7,000.

Sometimes, after residents complain about a chemical release, the refinery people go door-to-door offering each person in the house fifty dollars to sign off on a sheet saying their complaint was satisfied. Of course, people are going to take that money. Fifty dollars is better than no dollars. There go your rights.

Once hot, now cold

You have to watch out for a person who was once hot, but now they're cold. This is because industry offers people money to shut up. If you really need $3,000 or $4,000, you might think, "Hmm…I could pay a lot of bills with that. I have to feed my family. OK, I tell you what, give it to me and I'll keep my mouth closed. I'll lighten it up a little bit."

I was offered money myself: $4,000 and four computers for the center we started. I told them, "I'd love to have it. Sure, we need the money, but if you are doing this because you want me to drop the contested hearing I filed for, you can forget it because it is not going to happen. We need the cash, but I don't want it so bad I'm going to sell out my community."

They said, "That's really not why we'd give you the money. We would like to give you this money because this is what we do. We like to help projects out in the community. We'll call you. We'll make contact."

That was three and a half years ago. I'm still waiting.

Some people will settle for a thousand, five thousand, or ten thousand dollars. What are you going to do with that, for a whole community? Ten thousand dollars won't get a community center up and running. We need money to build a medical center, to keep the medication coming in to treat the asthma that these kids have. We need an emergency shelter in the event of an accident at the chemical plants and three emergency vans to pick people up and get them out of the community. That is twelve million dollars.

Community advisory panel

The refineries have community advisory panels and they select well-to-do folks to be on the panels. They know the panel members are content with what they have because they don't even live in the community. The refinery guys say, "We have people here representing the community and they say everything's fine." That's not the real community.

When the panel meets, they have their little box lunches, they talk about what's going on at the plant, and then they go home. No one sitting on that panel brings up the issue of pollution and what needs to be done. That is why I couldn't be on that panel. I went to a couple of their meetings, with all the refinery heads and all these people I grew up with, my teachers, clergymen, people that I had respected. I said, "You know what's going on and you're just sitting there."

Improvement so far

As a result of our work, the companies are starting to rethink their approach. Premcor, for instance, has installed a couple of new units and changed the burners on some of their heaters. BASF has started to change their units to recover some of the chemicals they otherwise would have spewed into the air.

Due to these and other changes, the plants have reduced their rate of emissions. If they had stayed the same size they were ten years ago, the amount of emissions would be down by 15-20%, but because they keep adding production capacity, they are dumping the same total amount of chemicals into the air.[3]

Flaring is down by 20-25%. Whenever those flares go off there's a heavy rumbling with smoke pouring off and we call our state regulatory agency every time. The agency, in turn, has started to issue violation notices and fines. The refineries are still dumping gasses into the air, because we still have sulfur odors, but it is not as frequent as it used to be. Everybody knows it's due to our work, and they really appreciate it.

In a 2004 lawsuit settlement, we won two newly invented toxic air monitors that tell users instantly how much of what chemicals are in the air. The monitor can detect 20 volatile organic and industrial compounds. I have traveled all over the United States with this monitor, helping other fenceline groups get a fix on what they are breathing. Along the way, I have helped build a national network of such groups, and we are teaching one another the lessons we've learned.

I'm enjoying myself and I've learned a lot. There is nothing more rewarding than standing up for people who are not strong enough to stand up for themselves and having some victories. Every time I look at a little child outside in the park playing, I know they're not breathing as much poison as they would be had it not been for our group fighting.

---

3. It's a gray area because the government lets them trade 'pollution credits.' If one industry is slated to dump so many thousands of pounds of chemicals into the air, and they do not use all that, another company can buy that credit and dump over their limit. It's a shell game and the people living on the fenceline are still getting dangerous doses of chemicals.

Only for a short while

Hilton Kelley

Many seasons will come
Many seasons will go
Have you ever tried to fly? Have you ever tried to grow?
Do you sit in your comfort zone waiting for tomorrow
A time that will never come because you're drowning in your
    sorrow
Searching for the perfect time in which to make your move
Making plans with in your mind to no one must you prove
How far it is you wish to fly
Before your final sigh
If you stand up and give it just one last try,
You just might put a spark back in someone's eye
Giving them the courage to try
Giving them the courage to fly
Giving hope where there was none
Bringing them pride
Bringing them sun
Shining light up on darkness to help them find their way
Never from the road will any of them stray
Missing all the pits that one can hit in a day
Flying high up in the sky
Never becoming prey
To those who wish to destroy them
Because they know the way
Have you ever tried to fly? Have you ever tried to grow?
Many season will come many season will go.

Dedicated to Community In-power and Development Association core members: Lydia, Billy, Stephen, Virgie, Tashiica, Archie, Tony, Shereena Broddrick, Markeeta, Muffin, Linda, Rev. James, Rev. Malveaux, Rev. Abram, Erica and Eryca, Rev. Dominic, Kenneth, Johnny, Shanta, Denny, Anne and Ann, Michael, Nyelle, and Flip.

©Hilton Kelley, May 8, 2004.

CHAPTER 2

▼

A LITTLE HOMEWORK

Rachael Belz

Preparing for a good neighbor campaign includes a little homework to size up the company and the neighborhood.

Let's talk about a series of techniques that have worked for us at Ohio Citizen Action, with the example of a good neighbor campaign in the North Avondale neighborhood of Cincinnati.

A local company, Cincinnati Specialties, was manufacturing flavorings, rust inhibitors, specialty chemicals, and noxious odors. It was discharging toxic methanol into the city sewers and had had seventeen accidental chlorine releases in nine years. Cincinnati Specialties officials estimated that a full-scale chlorine accident at the plant could affect one million people.

After the 1999-2000 good neighbor campaign, the company eliminated the methyl anthranilate odor, built an enclosure building to prevent accidents from chlorine-laden rail cars, and began running an improved methanol recovery unit.

1. Sizing up the company

At first, the neighbors did not even know where the odors were coming from. They knew something smelled awful in St. Bernard, a small town bordering the North Avondale neighborhood. The town had a number of factories, including Procter and Gamble, Cognis Chemical, Cincinnati Vulcan Lubricants, and Cincinnati Specialties.

From the 1980s to the early 1990s, the neighbors suspected that the smell was coming from Procter and Gamble, but they were not sure. The neighbors asked for tours of several facilities. Cincinnati Specialties turned them down, but when they toured Procter and Gamble, they found no smells there. The situation did not add up.

Then the neighbors started learning a little about each company. They found out that Cincinnati Specialties made flavorings. This matched the grape smell they had been complaining about, and they thought, "It might be these guys."

In other cases, a clue can come from comparing each company's hours of operation to when the smells are in the air. Do they operate twenty-four hours a day, seven days a week, or are they a five-day-a-week operation? Maybe the company you suspect is not open on the weekend, and there is another company behind them that is open 24/7.

Once neighbors had gathered enough evidence to satisfy themselves that the problem was coming from Cincinnati Specialties, they started to assemble all the information they could find about it. The steps they followed can be used in any campaign.

Neighbors' memories

Start with the neighbors' own memories. In the Cincinnati Specialties campaign, some knew the company had had a chlorine leak in the late 1980s. It was so bad that nearby Procter and Gamble sent their employees home.

A visit to the local fire department to talk with responders and examine records showed that Cincinnati Specialties was still having problems with chlorine leaks. Since the fire department was located adjacent to Cincinnati Specialties' property, the responders even stated that "sometimes they would smell the chlorine even before they'd received the call from Cincinnati Specialties."

We figured that chlorine is a chemical that many companies use. Most often, it is delivered in railcars. We'd heard that the Clorox plant in Cleveland had built a chlorine enclosure building about fifteen years earlier. I made an appointment to see it. The administrative manager on site, John Jurcsisn, asked me more about why I was so interested in this building. I explained about our work with Cincinnati Specialties and the chlorine problems they had. He said he was willing to share anything with me that might be helpful.

When I arrived, Mr. Jurcsisn gave me an extensive tour of the enclosure building and the plant. He showed me how even a little puff of chlorine released would automatically shut off the production line, slam the outside doors of the enclosure building, causing the enclosure building to go under "negative pressure." That way, not one drop of the chlorine released would escape outside. There was a scrubber or two associated with the enclosure building too.

Afterwards, Mr. Jurcsisn gave me a binder with all of the information as well as manufacturers they had used when they built their enclosure building. He told me that he'd be willing to work with Cincinnati Specialties and even be willing to trade plant tours with them so he might see it for himself. This was my first concrete example as to how different the "corporate culture" can be from company to company, plant to plant.

At the next meeting with the neighbors, we gave the plant manager all of the information about Clorox's enclosure building. They were interested. The plants traded tours, and eventually Cincinnati Specialties built their own chlorine enclosure building. They reduced the risk to their workers and neighbors, found a way to detect and control leaks before they happen, and made the community happy.

Internet

Once you have tapped everyone's memories, turn to the internet. Of course, you do not have to learn how to do internet research yourself if you can find somebody to help. It may be another neighbor, one of your kids, or anyone who knows the basics. Start by entering the name of the company into a Google search, and see what pops up. Of course, the information that appears is only as reliable as its source, so be as skeptical as always and keep careful notes.

Once you have gleaned some general information, look at the Toxics Release Inventory data.[1] Start with the list of chemicals the company emits and see how much of each they released, in pounds. One of the chemicals on the list may be causing the odor, but the report will not say, for example, "grape flavorings, 2,000 pounds." It may say "methyl anthranilate."

You can search the database back to 1988, the first year for Toxics Release Inventory reports. This will give you a little more company his-

---

1. The Toxics Release Inventory reports annual toxic chemical releases of 650 different chemicals by certain industries and federal facilities. In 1984 a deadly cloud of methyl isocyanate killed thousands of people in Bhopal, India; it was followed by a large chemical release at a sister plant in West Virginia. In reaction, grassroots groups across the country demanded and won the creation of the Inventory in the 1986 Emergency Planning and Community Right-to-Know Act, expanded in 1990. This database is on the RTK-NET website is maintained by OMB Watch in Washington, D.C. (http://www.rtk.net). "RTK" stands for "right to know." You can also get this information from the U.S. EPA website, http://www.epa.gov/tri/.

tory. Has the company gotten rid of any chemicals? Does it seem as though they have changed their product line?

In 1990, most companies reported a dramatic decrease in emissions because they did not want to be the worst polluter on the list. This is why many companies like to compare their current numbers to 1988 numbers. They want to show a big decrease. They might say, "Since 1988, we've reduced our emissions of this chemical by 85%." You might reply, "I know, but 84% of that reduction came in 1990. Since then you've only come down by 1%, and that was only because your product wasn't selling."

Every July 1, companies have to report their previous year's emissions to the U.S. EPA. Then, the agency takes six to twelve months to put that information into a giant database. That is why at the end of 2005, the most recent data available was from 2003. Even though it is a couple of years old, it is worth looking at this information. Unless there has been a big change or sale of the company, what they did in 2003 is probably close to what they are doing now.

This is where it gets interesting. You are now looking at what they released in 2003, the year before that and the year before that.[2] The reports also list what companies plan to release in the next two years. If these planned releases are roughly the same as the actuals for the last reporting year, you can see that they are not planning to make improvements.

Two more good sources of information about specific companies are the U.S. EPA's Enforcement and Compliance History Online, sometimes called "ECHO," and RTK-NET's collection of company "risk management plan" summaries.[3]

---

2. Since you do not want to wait two years to get last year's numbers, contact your state environmental agency air office on July 1 to pick up a copy of last year's numbers. As soon as the company submits it, it is public information, and you can make a copy of it. Keep in mind these are the raw numbers, and they may change slightly as the U.S. EPA processes them. In my experience, these numbers rarely change, but if you use them in the campaign, note that these are raw unofficial company numbers.

The last internet research task is to consult the Scorecard website, which tells what each chemical can do to the human body.[4] Other people can help you with this as well, including a doctor, especially an occupational doctor, a teacher at the local community college, or a chemist who lives in the neighborhood.

Library

Now you can shut down the computer, because it is time to go to the library to research your local newspapers. Librarians are quite helpful with this kind of research. Back issues may be on-line, in hard copy, or on microfiche or microfilm archives. In addition to copying key articles, it helps to make yourself a simple timeline of events in the company history.

While you are there, ask the librarian to help you find basic information about the company. Who are the chief executive officer and the plant manager? Where is the corporate headquarters? Do stockholders own the company or is it privately held (family-owned)? Is the company making money or losing money? You need to know, because you are going to be asked.

Government agencies

Even if your local regulatory agencies don't do much regulating, they can be a great source of information for you. In the Cincinnati Specialties campaign, we took our questions to the local air agency, called the Hamilton County Department of Environmental Services, and the Metropolitan Sewer District.

Local air agencies can be right in your neighborhood or two hours away. They can be a part of city or county government or a multi-county regional agency.

You will find that the agency staff dealing with air pollution typically are not the staff responsible for water pollution or sewers. In fact, they may

---

3. ECHO can be found at http://www.epa.gov/echo/and the RTK-NET collection is at http://www.rtknet.org/rmp/.
4. The Scorecard website, created by Environmental Defense, is now managed by the Green Media Toolshed: http://www.scorecard.org

be in three separate agencies. Often these officials do not even talk to one another. When you talk to them about all the problems at a company, it may be the first time they have learned the full scope of the problem.

Talking to Sewer District officials was important in the Cincinnati Specialties campaign because the company was dumping lots of toxic waste into the sewers. Cincinnati has combined sanitary and rainwater sewers, a problem now being fixed at a cost of $1.5 billion. Until the fix is complete, if a company releases hazardous chemicals into the sewer system, and a storm causes it to overflow, the waste is not going to make it to the water treatment plant. The company does not know and does not care. Once the waste is gone, it is gone. The treatment plant does not know and does not care. They get what they get.

If your research shows that the smells do not match up with the chemicals in the Toxics Release Inventory, the company's emissions fee report can help.[5] This report covers releases of large and small particulates, sulfur dioxide, nitrogen oxide, carbon monoxide, organic compounds, volatile organic compounds, mercury, lead, arsenic, and benzene.[6] These reports are usually not available on line, but you can get them from local agencies. The state agency has copies as well, but the local agency will have the most up to date information.

---

5. The emissions fee report may be called the emissions inventory or something slightly different in other states.

6. "Particulates" are what the U.S. EPA calls soot. "Volatile organic compounds": "Organic chemicals all contain the element carbon (C); organic chemicals are the basic chemicals found in living things and in products derived from living things, such as coal, petroleum and refined petroleum products. Many of the organic chemicals we use do not occur in Nature, but were synthesized by chemists in laboratories. Volatile chemicals produce vapors readily; at room temperature and normal atmospheric pressure, vapors escape easily from volatile liquid chemicals. Volatile organic chemicals include gasoline, industrial chemicals such as benzene, solvents such as toluene and xylene, and tetrachloroethylene (perchloroethylene, the principal dry cleaning solvent). Many volatile organic chemicals are also hazardous air pollutants; for example, benzene causes cancer," U.S. EPA.

You can get the emissions fee report as soon as the company files it. In Ohio, it is usually due April 15 for the previous year's emissions. As with the Toxics Release Inventory, I always check reports for the last five years.

The report is usually one or two pages of emission numbers broken down by process. The processes are not named. Instead, just a permit number appears, for example "B-1027." This number will match up with one part of the facility. For example, B-1027 may be a boiler. When you are at the local agency, ask them to give you a copy of the code sheet explaining what each means. The figures will be in tons rather than pounds.[7]

Recently, all air pollution permits for each company have been consolidated into one and it must be renewed every five years. This consolidation makes it easier for the companies and the citizens. You can just go get the one permit for the whole company and figure out what problem you need to address. It is also easier for neighbors to come and say their piece at one big hearing rather than dozens of little ones. Since Title V of the federal Clean Air Act Amendments of 1990 required the air pollution permits, some people call them "Title V permits," or just "Title V."

When you are at the local air agency, you can find out what the agency knows about the company. If you know somebody who is familiar with environmental paperwork, ask him or her to come with you, or contact a group to see about free technical assistance. If you try to do it all yourself, you may be overwhelmed quickly by the technical jargon.

You have to make an appointment. You will go in, and they will probably put you in a room and ask what files you want. You may say you want all of them for that company. If so, they have to comply. Plan to be there for a few hours or, if you are investigating a large company, a few days.

Generally, the bigger the company, the more files there will be, whether they are a bad company or not. On the other hand, no matter what the size of the company, the more problems they have had, the more files they are going to have. So, if a little chemical company with 200 employees has a big stack of files, something has been going on there.

---

7. 1 ton = 2,000 pounds.

For me, the most helpful files to start with are the least technical. I first look at citizen complaints. I want a copy of any complaint from anybody else in my town this year, or in some cases, going back five years.

Even if only a handful of people have complained, do not get discouraged. I know from experience that for every person who complained, there are dozens, or maybe hundreds, of other people who smelled it.

You will probably have to pay for copies, although many agencies will give you the first 200 or 250 free. Ask them up front, and get as many free copies as possible. Some agencies charge between five and twenty-five cents a copy. You should argue with them if they charge more than five cents; do not just take it sitting down. Most states have a policy that agencies can only charge for the paper and machine wear-and-tear, about five cents a copy, but not for personnel time.

Even if you end up having to pay more, the ones you want to pay for are those citizen complaints. They are gold. The records have the complainant's name and phone number, and a little bit about the complaint. You can just call all the people on the list and stop by their houses.[8]

The agency is also required to keep copies of all correspondence. Since much of it is in plain English, you can learn the relationship between the agency and company, and what shapes the regulators opinions of the company. If the company has been a real problem for the agency, with repeated violations or letters from their lawyers, make a note of this. In the Cincinnati Specialties Campaign, the correspondence told us the company had a rough relationship with the Metropolitan Sewer District, so we consistently stressed sewer issues, and regularly checked up on the company at the Sewer District.

Sometimes the correspondence files show the company running things past the agency, such as whether to install new equipment. Even if they ditch the idea before they get to the permit stage, the correspondence tips you off to the potential issue and that the company wants to do something about it.

---

8. You may find that the complaint file contains nothing useful, because some agencies, like Toledo Environmental Services, do not write the names and addresses of complainants down. This is inexcusable.

Citizen audit

Lastly, save all your research, because once the campaign is underway, you may want to issue a citizen audit of the plant. A citizen audit puts down in one place all the information you have gathered about the company, including what you have learned at the regulatory agencies, information from websites, surveys, interviews, whistleblowers, newspapers, and library research. The audit might have full recommendations, minimal recommendations, or none at all. You can issue the audit as a paper report and post it on your website if you have one.

This tactic has many advantages. Writing it helps clarify your thinking about what is wrong. It is a great resource for reporters first learning about the campaign. It establishes your credibility, since you obviously do your homework. If you uncover newsworthy information, it may make the news. Since at least one person at the company, and probably many more, will definitely read it, it helps them think about how they could improve.

Preparing it is time-consuming, however, so it is best done as a side project of the campaign. Do not suspend your public activities to do the audit, or things will get too quiet for too long. You should only undertake this project if you have the help of a volunteer who is used to reading environmental data and reports.

In some circumstances, an audit may not be a good idea. Sometimes, you just cannot get enough information about the company to describe it accurately. A pending environmental lawsuit may keep you from getting necessary documents. In other cases, there may be too much information, as with a big company. Unless you have a big organizational partner that can offer considerable technical assistance, there may be too much to digest.

2. Sizing up the neighborhood

What do we have in common?

As you think about putting together a group, start with yourself. What do I care about? What do my family and friends care about? What do I know about my community? Maybe, even though I grew up here, I have never considered what other people think about these issues.

What do we have in common? Do not stop with just one or two things. We are all residents, we all vote, and we all pay taxes here. That is a start, but what else?

For instance, if a neighborhood, a small town, or a small city is deeply religious and many people attend church regularly, then one of the first things on your list may be talking to your own church leaders, and then contacting other churches. If three-quarters of the people go to church, where do they go? What, if anything, does it mean for the campaign that everybody's kids go to the same elementary school?

Many people have lived here for a long time and have a lot of history and knowledge they do not realize is valuable to the campaign.

If you know that asthma rates are higher than normal, talk with people about it. You may want to ask, "Do you happen to know that there is a big problem with asthma in our community?" Maybe that will connect with them. "You're not sick, but your son has asthma. Maybe you never really thought about why, because so many kids have asthma now."

"Oh, it's a childhood thing, just one of those things children go through. They'll grow out of it." Some kids do grow out of it, some do not, and some kids move away from the chemicals that trigger their asthma.

Let's talk about the stench from the company. It is what everybody smells at the soccer fields. I would talk to the soccer moms. They are sick of it, but nobody knows what to do about it. By the way, the company leases the land for a dollar to the town so nobody is going to complain.

The neighbors and the workers

Unless you want to shut the facility down, you want to make clear from the very beginning that you do not want to shut it down. Do this because it will come at you no matter what. It is much better to head this issue off at the pass. People will always ask this, especially in small towns and cities, or tight-knit neighborhoods. "It's the tax base." "My dad works there." Your answer is, "We're working to protect him, too." The changes these campaigns seek are good for the whole community, including the workers. Unfortunately, however, the company often tries to pit neighbors against workers.

The choice is not between the company venting pollution onto the workers inside the building or outside into the community. That is no answer. It is not a trade-off. The solution has to be good for neighbors and workers.

You are not a union representative negotiating worker issues, but if you make the plant cleaner, it is practically impossible for it not to be safer for workers. There is just that much more scrutiny of that leaky valve.

Will the plant have to spend money to do this? Probably, but often that is money that they have not been spending to maintain it, or money they are spending anyway on less effective solutions to the problem.

When this question comes up, with neighbors or the company, it is important that you do not feel like you have to have all the answers. That is why you work with the company. There are usually people somewhere in the company who already know what needs to be done.

You may meet people with technical expertise. A neighbor may also be a nurse, a teacher, a chemist, or an engineer. Sometimes the best ally on a campaign has been a neighbor who works at a different company, and has become an expert there on how to prevent pollution. They know maintenance is important. They know what these chemicals can do if you dump them down the drain.

They do not have to be fenceline neighbors like you happen to be. They could be just interested people who come to the table because their kid goes to school across the street, even though they live two miles away. If they are interested in what you are doing and they want to be involved, go for it.

The starting five

Find at least five neighbors from different backgrounds who agree with you about the problem. Once you have found the starting five, have a meeting. Five people are a good number to start with because you usually have one or two leader types who can get people motivated.

Then you have one or two people who can help you do some of the research, maybe someone who knows computers. Maybe someone has a schedule that allows them to go down to the agency. Someone else is a local leader in the PTA, their church, or a block watch. Work with them to think about all the different ways people can bring something to the table, even though they may not realize it.

The stay-at-home mom of the group probably knows more moms in the neighborhood than anybody else does. She is more valuable than almost any other member you might have. People who might feel that they are out of the game can be some of the best activists in the neighborhood, simply because they are there. A day-care mom may be there all day long, taking care of her own kids and three other families' kids two blocks from the facility. She smells it no matter what time of day it is. The kids go out to play in the back yard, and they shout, "It stinks!" She is more valuable than someone who goes away for ten hours a day to his or her job.

Your goal does not need to be to build the group to hundreds of people. In fact, if that happened, managing it would be difficult. It would be a full-time job. You can just go with the five. If you want it to be bigger, you could shoot for fifteen to twenty people. That would be ideal. It is not too big that people cannot host meetings in their house. It is enough people so that if someone wants to drop back for a while, or have something going on with their family, they can do it without disrupting the campaign.

You might as well prepare for the fact that the group is going to ebb and flow. Not everybody is going to make the same time commitment. The longer you are dealing with the company before the changes are made, the more change there will be in your own group. There will be changes in their lives. People will join, people will drop off, and everybody will have good reasons.

As the beginning of your campaign approaches, your group's discussions should get increasingly sober. Anne Rolfes, founding director of the Louisiana Bucket Brigade, has met with many community groups thinking of beginning a good neighbor campaign.

The first step is getting in there, taking the temperature of the neighborhood, and figuring out if they really have the wherewithal and the leadership of people who have savvy. You can be interested and committed, but if you are going to be bought off by the first offer from the refinery, it is not really worth the time. That is the first step, figuring out if people have the gumption and the commitment for it.

The second step is working with people to figure out what their goal is, what the community wants, and making sure they can stick to that. A number of communities in Louisiana have been fighting these battles for a long time. They have gotten some things done, gotten publicity or attended many hearings, but they haven't actually won anything. It is because they have never decided on a goal. Some places are surrounded by twenty different companies, and we cannot go after all of them. They will not pick one company, or even one issue. You have to pick one of something, as hard as that is. There have been many places we have not been able to work with because they will not focus. There is no way we can win if we are going to be responding to everything.

The third step is engaging the company by sending a letter [inviting the company to meet], with a deadline. No company has ever met with us at first. We have had to drag them through the mud for years. It will be good when they start to meet with us to begin with.

Then, if they won't engage, the fourth step is launching the public campaign.[9]

---

9. Anne Rolfes (Founding Director, Louisiana Bucket Brigade), interview by Paul Ryder, Cleveland, Ohio, July 21, 2005.

CHAPTER 3

▼

HOW A CAMPAIGN

UNFOLDS

Paul Ryder

Once launched, the good-neighbor campaign typically goes through two stages. In the first stage, the company refuses to treat the neighbors as neighbors. If they talk to them at all, it is not serious and little is accomplished. The pollution continues unabated. After months or years, however, a turning point arrives when the company decision-maker changes his mind and begins to talk in earnest with the neighbors. This begins the second stage, described in Chapter 10.

1. What makes a company executive change his mind?

Everyone has a conscience. What is inside it varies from person to person, but it always includes the Golden Rule. This precept is taught by every religion in the world, as the following examples illustrate:

- Hinduism: "This is the sum of duty: do not do to others what would cause pain if done to you."

- Buddhism: "Treat not others in ways that you yourself would find hurtful."

- Taoism: "Regard your neighbour's gain as your own gain and your neighbour's loss as your own loss."

- Confucianism: "Do not do to others what you do not want done to yourself."

- Judaism: "What is hateful to you, do not do to your neighbor. This is the whole Torah; all the rest is commentary. Go and learn it."

- Christianity: "In everything, do to others as you would have them do to you; for this is the law and the prophets."

- Islam: "Not one of you truly believes until you wish for others what you wish for yourself."[1]

Outside of religion, every serious moral or ethical code is also based on the Golden Rule. This is one thing human beings have agreed on.

It does not mean, of course, that everyone practices the Golden Rule all the time. It does mean that violations of it are indefensible. To violate it is to defy the values of your mom and dad, six billion other people now alive, and all your ancestors going back thousands of years. That is quite a burden for anyone to take on.

What could be a clearer violation of the Golden Rule than putting toxic chemicals in a community's air and water? The list of the most despicable crimes has always included poisoning the town well. That is what polluters do.

This moral factor is by far the most important reason why good neighbor campaigns succeed.

In addition, each company has its own weaknesses. The neighbors group should discuss these and agree on a list of the three or four most important ones. The list should be simple enough that you can put it on a 4" x 6" index card.

Here is what appeared on the index card of possible AK Steel weaknesses:

aggressiveness
inability to control every porch conversation
size of city
dominates Middletown

"Aggressiveness" referred to our sense that AK Steel CEO Richard Wardrop's well-known belligerence may have started to turn self-destructive. "Dominates Middletown" meant that AK Steel managers may have mistakenly assumed that Middletown was a safe company town, and that they could take their neighbors for granted.

Once you have your index card, start experimenting with tactics that bring the moral factor to bear. Many of the best tactics simply aim to edu-

---

1. *Mahabharata* 5:1517; The Buddha, *Udana-Varga* 5.18; Lao Tzu, *T'ai Shang Kan Ying P'ien*, 213-218; Confucius, *Analects* 15.23; Hillel, *Talmud*, Shabbath 31a; Jesus, *Matthew* 7:12; and The Prophet Muhammad, *Hadith*. Translations by Paul McKenna, Scarboro Missions, 2685 Kingston Rd., Scarborough, ON, Canada M1M 1M4, interfaith@scarboromissions.ca.

cate as many people as possible about what the pollution is doing to people's health.

A good example of a tactic comes from Italy's *Legambiente* (Environmental League). To draw attention to industrial soot, the group distributed white flags for members to hang out their windows. Before long, the white flags turned gray. This was a good tactic because it was simple, cheap, fun, and got people involved. Its meaning was clear to all.

There are hundreds of tactics you can use, and people like you are inventing new ones all the time. The best place to get new ideas is from people in the neighborhood. To help prompt your imagination, you may want to consult the descriptions and examples of 200 tactics in Gene Sharp's book, *The Politics of Nonviolent Action*.[2]

Some tactics are described elsewhere in this handbook, including citizen audits (Chapter 2), door-knocking and house meetings (Chapter 5), logbooks and air sampling (Chapter 6), media (Chapter 8), and community health surveys (Appendix A).

When you start experimenting with tactics, of course you do not know which ones are going to work. Do not prejudge them; let the experiments give you the answer. If a tactic does not catch on, stop it immediately and try something different. If a tactic does catch on, pour all your resources into it.[3]

As these tactics educate more people, it should be possible to bring in more friends and neighbors. Never stop; the more the better.

At the same time, it is especially effective to add new allies from unexpected new directions.

- If a campaign has been led by a group on the plant's west side, invite an east side group to join the fray.

- If the local newspaper had been silent on the problem for years, persuade them to run an article on the plant's pollution. After a few articles, they may be ready to run an editorial.

---

2. Gene Sharp, *The Politics of Nonviolent Action* (Boston: Porter Sargent, 1973).
3. For more on this approach, see the chapter "Tactics dictate strategy," in Al Reis and Jack Trout, *Bottom-Up Marketing* (New York: Plume, 1990).

- If the plant employees have a union, make the union an early ally.

- In 2002, Gahanna, Ohio, neighbors took on Columbus Steel Drum, which cleans 5,000 hazardous waste drums a day. Among the most powerful neighbors was next door. The McGraw-Hill Company was fed up with the stench and occasional evacuations due to toxic emissions, and had to buy a new ventilation system to keep its employees safe. By the time the good neighbor campaign started, McGraw-Hill had already filed with the court a notice of intent to sue Columbus Steel Drum.

- In the same campaign, 733 neighbors wrote to Honda of America, a major customer of Columbus Steel Drum, urging the automaker to intervene. Since Honda sells its products directly to the consumer, and has invested in a "green" image, it was far more sensitive to consumer pressure than was Columbus Steel Drum. Honda responded immediately, got involved and reported back to the neighbors, "...we have periodically met to discuss Columbus Steel Drum's ongoing environmental issues directly with Columbus Steel Drum management. At these meetings, we have reviewed Columbus Steel Drum's operations and their compliance status, and we have encouraged Columbus Steel Drum to work with the appropriate government agencies and their neighbors in order to put their environmental compliance issues behind them."[4] Honda's intervention scared Columbus Steel Drum badly, and contributed to the neighbors' victory.

- Another kind of new ally is an organization with significant resources. Greenpeace was just such an ally when Norco, Louisiana, neighbors took on Shell Oil.

"'The role played by Greenpeace was crucial because Greenpeace is big enough and has enough money that it can commit to a struggle

---

4. Karen Heyob, Environmental Manager, Honda of America, letter to Simona Vaclavikova, Columbus Program Director, Ohio Citizen Action, May 2, 2003.

for a long period of time,' said Beverly Wright. 'Often, fenceline industries are able to simply outlast the energies and resources of local community activists, but once Greenpeace takes on a battle there is a new equation and enough resources to see the struggle through,' she added."[5]

The less expected the new ally is, the better. It means you have changed the landscape a little. You have given the company something new to take into account. Add another unexpected ally a month later, and then another.

After a while, company executives who once thought time was on their side are not so sure. Maybe things are getting a little out of control. Maybe the future is not so predictable. Top management starts talking about the need to "get ahead of this issue."

One of your surprising new allies can be the company executive's own conscience.

To repeat: Everyone has a conscience.

For a moment, look through the eyes of the CEO or plant manager. He has worked his way into a corner and does not know how to get out. He knows that what he has been doing is wrong. He wants to stop but does not know how. He has been avoiding the matter so completely that he really does not know how bad it is. He has been denying the problem for years, so it is harder to acknowledge it now. Since it is indefensible, he wants to avoid thinking or talking about it. He does not want to be yelled at by neighbors, some of whom look like his mom (who taught him the Golden Rule in the first place). He does not want to lose his job. He does not want to appear weak by giving in to the neighbors, or by outright losing to them.

5. Steve Lerner, *Diamond: A Struggle for Environmental Justice in Louisiana's Chemical Corridor* (Cambridge, Massachusetts: MIT Press, 2005), 201-202. Beverly Wright is executive director of the Deep South Center for Environmental Justice, now at Dillard University in New Orleans.

It is not in our interest for him to stay in that corner, because as long as he does, we will keep breathing and drinking his toxic waste. How can we help him get out of the corner?

Help the executive learn how bad it is.

This can be done even if he refuses to talk directly with you.

You can send him handwritten letters. Such letters are unusual these days, and the odds are he will want to read them, or at least a sample of them.[6]

If the pollution includes asthma-triggering chemicals, you can use a simple drinking straw to help the executive experience asthma first-hand. In 2005, neighbors of the giant Mittal Steel complex in Cleveland, Ohio, signed slips that said the following:

> Dear Mr. Mittal [Company CEO Lakshmi Mittal]:
>
> Please breathe through this straw for 60 seconds to see what it is like to have asthma. Pollutants from the Mittal Cleveland Works aggravate asthma for the 390,000 people who live within five miles of the plant. Did you know that this plant's emissions of sulfur dioxide and small particles, which can trigger asthma, increased by 38% from 2003 to 2004? It is time for you to invest in modernizing the Cleveland Works Plant to prevent pollution.

A single drinking straw was taped to each note. In June 2005, a local student traveling to England delivered 458 of these messages and straws to Lakshmi Mittal's London headquarters. This tactic was easy to do and quite cheap; straws cost one-half cent each.

You can videotape interviews with neighbors describing what life is like for them in the shadow of the plant. The interviews can be copied to VHS tape or DVD and sent to the decision-maker.

Of course, just sending something does not guarantee that the executive will look at it. Something else will take care of that: if he keeps refusing to communicate with you, send a copy of everything to each member of his

---

6. See Chapter 8 for more on letters.

board of directors. As a matter of his own bureaucratic survival, every CEO insists on seeing everything his board sees.

Show him how neighbors resolve problems with one another.

If you want him to be open, honest and respectful to you, that is how you should deal with him. If you want him to be trustworthy with you, be that way yourself.

When you speak, what is coming across about you? Are you someone who seeks to divide people or unite them? Are you someone who wants an unconditional surrender from the company, or are you a genuine community leader?[7]

Speak directly to the best in him, his conscience.

Anne Rolfes mentions two Louisiana community leaders who speak to conscience:

> That's definitely how Margie Richard worked in Norco. She was not coming out with guns blazing at all, ever. She was always appealing to their conscience. She used to say over and over, 'When are you going to do what's right for the people? When are you going to do what's right?' Ken Ford in Chalmette is the same in a way. He's not so directly religious or so directly speaking about people's conscience, but he does not have his guns blazing. He just won't do it. I think that is effective. It's strong and not belligerent. That's how a lot of successful people are doing it.[8]

---

7. The good-neighbor approach differs from orthodox community organizing, which personally attacks 'targets' with ridicule and humiliation and stages degrading 'accountability sessions.' Promoted by Saul Alinsky (1909-1967) and his followers, the orthodox approach is one reason why community organizing has not come close to realizing its potential in this country.
8. Anne Rolfes (Founding Director, Louisiana Bucket Brigade), interview with author, Cleveland, Ohio, July 21, 2005.

It may seem fanciful (or worse) to put a CEO's conscience in your campaign plan, until you have seen the remarkable results that can come from it.

The results do not come immediately, and you may only get clues at first. Other times, it is clear. During one recent campaign, in the middle of a contentious meeting, a CEO commented to a neighbors' representative, "I have never felt worse about anything than I do about what's going on in this community." A good outcome followed shortly.[9]

One objection to this approach is that it may work with some CEOs, "but not with the one we've got here. He's a real so-and-so."

This brings us back to the case of Richard Wardrop, who was AK Steel CEO when a good neighbor campaign began in 2001.[10] He was famous throughout the industry for his over-the-top hostility to customers, suppliers, competitors, neighbors, employees and government officials at all levels. Neighbors throughout the region sent him 24,000 handwritten letters urging him to do something about pollution from his Middletown Works. At the 2002 AK Steel shareholders meeting, Wardrop denied receiving any letters at all.

Neighbors decided that awakening Wardrop's conscience was taking a long time and that they should bring other people's consciences into the equation. They began to write to AK Steel's board of directors. When the board learned how bad it was, they could have either tried to persuade Mr. Wardrop to change, or they could have replaced him. Faced with a shrinking stock price and a growing good neighbor campaign, the board decided to show Mr. Wardrop the door.

---

9. For more on the role of conscience in violent and non-violent conflict, see Richard Gregg, *The Power of Nonviolence* (Ahmedabad, India: Navajivan Publishing House, 1938, revised 1960).

10. AK Steel's Middletown Works had been spewing 11 million pounds each year of soot containing heavy metals. In all, it emitted 68 million pounds each year of air pollution, including carbon monoxide, sulfur dioxide, nitrogen oxide, volatile organic compounds and lead. PCB releases contaminated Dick's Creek, making it unsafe for fishing, swimming or wading.

His successor, James Wainscott, promptly started talking with the campaign. Before long, he began to invest $65 million in pollution prevention at the Middletown Works, which will cut soot emissions by at least 90%.

We leave it to others to debate whether, given enough time, Mr. Wardrop's conscience would have eventually got the better of him.

Lawyers

You will need to check out some tactics legally. For example, what if a whistleblower comes forward with "smoking gun" internal company documents, but wants to make sure that she won't get in legal trouble for giving them to you? What if you want to make sure you won't get in legal trouble for receiving them from her? You will need good legal advice.

Unfortunately, there is no association or referral service just for environmental plaintiffs' attorneys. Many attorneys describe themselves as environmental lawyers, but few of them work on behalf of environmental or citizens groups. Most local bar associations have environmental committees, and while there may be a few citizen lawyers in the ranks, most are stacked with industry lawyers.

A good place to start is to ask major state, regional, or national environmental groups what lawyers they have used and their track record. Another possible source is one of several law school environmental clinics.[11] Another possibility is Wildlaw, a non-profit environmental law firm with offices in Alabama, North Carolina, Florida, Virginia, and Utah.[12]

You can look up any attorney in the Martindale-Hubbell database to find their lawyer's rating and areas of practice, such as environmental law or Superfund litigation.[13] Contact the attorney by phone for an appoint-

---

11. Tulane Environmental Law Clinic, Weinmann Hall, 6329 Freret Street, New Orleans, LA 70118-6231, (504) 865-5939,http://www.tulane.edu/~telc/; Pacific Environmental Advocacy Center, Lewis & Clark Law School, 10015 S.W. Terwilliger Boulevard, Portland, Oregon 97219, (503) 768-6600, http://www.lclark.edu/org/peac/ Environmental Law Center, Vermont Law School, P.O. Box 96, Chelsea Street, South Royalton, VT 05068, (800) 227-1395; http://www.vermontlaw.edu/elc/index.cfm.
12. Sara O'Neal, Executive Director, Wildlaw, 8116 Old Federal Road, Suite C, Montgomery, Alabama 36117, (334) 396-4729, sara@wildlaw.org.

ment. Do not be afraid to ask about preliminary costs up front. In fact, make sure to ask all the tough awkward questions first.

Subcampaigns

These campaigns can last for years. It helps to break them up with a subcampaign, a campaign within a campaign that aims to resolve a specific sore point with the company.

For example, in the Rohm and Haas campaign in Reading, Ohio, one subcampaign addressed the problem of diesel trucks arriving at the plant in the middle of the night. Drivers let the trucks idle for hours, producing both air pollution and noise.

During the AK Steel campaign in Middletown, a subcampaign pressed the company to build a fence between Amanda Elementary School and Dick's Creek. The fence was needed to keep schoolchildren out of the creek, which was laced with PCBs from AK Steel.[14]

In the ISG/Mittal Steel plant campaign in Cleveland, a subcampaign took on a different truck problem. Dozens of times a day, uncovered trucks would roll down residential streets loaded with chunks of extremely hot coke. Baseball-sized pieces were bouncing off the trucks onto the streets, sidewalk and lawns, endangering neighbors and their children.

Subcampaigns are a great way to keep the initiative in a long campaign, give neighbors an interim victory and a sense of their power, and increase the campaign's engagement with the company. In a long campaign, you may pick up several subcampaign victories on your way to an overall solution.

---

13. Martindale Hubbell: http://www.martindale.com.
14. PCBs (polychlorinated biphenyls) are mixtures of synthetic organic chemicals used in electrical, heat transfer, and hydraulic equipment; in paints, plastics, rubber products, pigments, and dyes. In 1976, Congress banned PCBs, which can cause cancer, and attack the immune, hormone, reproductive and nervous systems.

2. Focus

Everyone thinks they know all they need to know about focus, but almost no one really does. For thousands of years, the wisest men and women have been trying to tell us that focus, concentration, is the key to success in every area of life: art, science, relationships, business, sports, spiritual life, politics, and so on.

You can prove this to yourself. Everyone has had a moment when they did something superbly. What was yours? Maybe you sang a song beautifully, or scored the winning goal, or saved someone from drowning, or comforted a child, or talked to God, or convinced a friend to do the right thing.

What was your state of mind at the time? Most people would say nothing was distracting them. Their surroundings, both sight and sound, faded. Time slowed down or maybe even stopped. They were focused.

Find someone who is the absolute best at what they do and ask them what it would take them to become even better. Odds are they will tell you that more focus, more concentration, would do it.

In the book *Focus*, Al Reis marches through the American economy, industry by industry, showing how focused companies have thrived and unfocused companies have come unglued.[15] The pattern is relentless, and business executives who have not noticed it have had their companies taken away from them. All the dynamics described in *Focus* also operate in non-profit groups, projects and campaigns.

The word "focus" originally referred to the ability of human eyes to see clearly one and only one object at a time. Other things may be visible in the background or peripherally, but they cannot be seen as clearly as the object in focus.

The meaning of the word has unfortunately degenerated. Too often, "focus" now means "put an item on my to-do list." It is common to hear someone announce, "Right now, we're focusing on four things."

15.*Focus*, Al Reis (New York: Collins, 1997).

Announcing it and doing it are not the same. If your eyes try to focus on four things at once, you are going to fall down the stairs.

Imagine that a friend meets you on the street and says, "So what is your group up to these days?" Often, the answer starts like this. "We're real busy. We are doing this and that and this…" And it turns into a stream of whatever is passing through your mind. What comes across is that you are completely unfocused.

If you had a focus, your answer would have showed it: "We're working on the community meeting on asthma. Did you get the invitation? Yeah, April 30. It's going to be really good. I'm glad I ran into you because there's a person on your street who needs a ride and I was hoping you could help with that."

It is hard to focus because it requires sacrifice. You have to make the hard decision that everything else is not the focus. That requires figuring out what you are doing, and it may disappoint people who want something else to be the focus.

For example, let's say your group is starting a letter-writing drive. Some people think the letters should go to the plant manager, and others think that the letters should go to the chief executive officer of the company.

It is tempting to take the easy way out, and decide that some people will write to one and some people will write to the other. Now you can announce, "We have a two-pronged strategy." It sounds like a good plan because you have used the words "prong" and "strategy." In fact, however, you are about to divide your scarce resources and be less effective, because you did not want to make the hard decision.

Two objections are sometimes raised to having a focus.

The first is, "Why hold back someone who can multi-task?" "Young people can multi-task and older people can't." "Women can multi-task and men can't."

Yes, you can juggle many things at once, but you are going to do a sloppy job on all of them. You will lose your campaign if you convince yourself that sloppy work is acceptable.

The second objection is that focusing is a good idea in theory, but in practice, there is just too much to do. On the contrary, focusing is the way to organize the campaign, given many tasks. Here's how, in four easy steps:

1. Identify a focus. Make the hard decision. For example, the focus might be stated as follows: "For the next two months, we are focusing on the public hearing." "For the next month we are focusing on building support for our campaign among area churches."

2. Now look at everything else on your list. Whenever possible, eliminate items that do not really need to be done at all. Then shrink the size of remaining items. Then delay items that do not absolutely need to be done now. With each of the remaining items, ask whether they can be delegated to others. A rule of organizing is that if someone else can do it, now or with a little training, they should do it. It is more than a rule. It is what organizing is all about. It's how you win.

3. What is left on the list is what absolutely has to be done now, and cannot be delegated. You, or someone in the core group, have to put it on their schedule.

4. All the rest of everyone's time goes to the focus.

Even if you start the campaign focused, it is easy to lose it over time. Ask yourselves regularly, "What is the focus right now?"

C H A P T E R 4

▼

THE INITIATIVE

Paul Ryder

1. Taking the initiative

Gandhi's most important contribution to the theory of nonviolence was his insistence that the resisters must keep the initiative at all times. While the opponent must be given ample opportunity to consider the proposals, he must not be allowed to ignore them. Gandhi fully understood that half the battle, indeed often the most difficult part of the battle, is to convince the opponent that he must deal with resisters.

Even in using force, the opponent becomes involved in a relationship with the movement and makes a commitment to resolving the issue.[1]

Taking the initiative means that you are taking the actions that define what the campaign is about. Everyone else is just reacting to your actions.

In sports, this is called "momentum." Teams that have the momentum in a game and keep it almost always win. The game is in their hands.

The other team is on the defensive, whether they are playing offense or defense. They are on their heels, off balance, struggling to regain their footing. They are losing.

Once you have the initiative, you can carry out your game plan. The trick is to do it at a pace that keeps everyone else scrambling to keep up with you. If you carry out your plan, but at too slow a pace, you are inviting trouble.

2. Losing the initiative

Like momentum in a game, initiative can be taken, lost, and taken again, many times during a campaign. What you want to do, of course, is to take the initiative at the beginning and never give it up.

Typically, it is not difficult for neighbors to take the initiative at the beginning of a good-neighbor campaign. Almost no one knows you exist, let alone takes you seriously. Once a campaign starts to succeed, however, others will want to take the initiative away from you.

You can lose the initiative and not know it. You can cruise for weeks, working hard, checking things off your checklist, before you realize something is wrong. Sometimes you can't put your finger on it, but you feel like the campaign is going uphill. Sometimes the clue is that you feel yourself buffeted by events.

The way to pin this down is to explicitly ask yourselves, every week or two: "Who has the initiative right now? Are we sure?"

---

1. Sanford Krolick, Betty Cannon, *Gandhi in the Postmodern Age*, Class on Nonviolence, Colman McCarthy, Center for Teaching Peace, 4501 Van Ness Street, NW, Washington, D.C. 20016 (202) 537-1372.

Sometimes you will conclude that no one has the initiative; that the issue is just drifting. This is a dangerous situation to be in, because it is easy for anyone to take the initiative. It is up for grabs.

In sports, there is only one team trying to take the momentum from you. In a good-neighbor campaign, there can be many others trying to take the initiative from you, sometimes all at the same time.

The following are some examples of how others can take the initiative from you if you are not careful.

The company's "Community Advisory Panel"

During the campaign, the company may set up a Community Advisory Panel if they do not already have one. If they are especially shameless, their public relations staff may write the following announcement:

> We thank the fenceline neighbors group for calling everyone's attention to this problem. You were right, and we are acting accordingly, doing just what you want. We are creating a Community Advisory Panel to work with our neighbors on solving this problem together. Of course, we will invite a responsible representative of the fenceline group to the meetings. We are confident that with this breakthrough, we can leave the finger-pointing behind us.

Sounds like you won, right? Not so fast. This is actually an attempt by the company to disorient you, divide the neighbors against one another, and create a process for slowly and quietly strangling your campaign.

Even neighbors who are well aware of this may not be sure how to handle the situation.

The key is understanding that the company is trying to take the initiative from you. If you try to stop it by complaining about what a fraud it is, you will be playing right into their hands. Why? It is because you are now reacting to their actions. By definition, you are yielding the initiative to them.

So, if we can't support the panel and we can't oppose it, what do we do? It depends on the circumstances, of course, but the general guidance for a time like this is to take the initiative right back, as described later in this chapter.

In the meantime, kick things up a notch or two by intensifying your current focus. Make it clear to the company that, instead of going away, your campaign is escalating. Whatever they do with their panel is irrelevant to you. They can have one or not, but things are going to keep getting more out of control until the company starts talking in good faith directly with you.

The company's scientists

Corporations also try to take the initiative by converting the issue into a scientific debate, a battle of experts sparring over obscure points. They know they are in the driver's seat when, for example, it becomes a dispute over whether two parts-per-billion or three parts-per-billion of a chemical is safe.

They have won because then only experts are left in the discussion, and the neighbors are left on the sidelines. Community leaders who try to be junior scientists and debate point after point unwittingly help the polluter do this.

There is a better way. These campaigns are really about values, not parts per billion. The word 'values' refers to what is important to us. You are the world expert on what is important to you. Who else but you can answer, for example, "Is a higher risk of my children getting cancer more or less important to me than the convenience of nonstick cookware?"

Science is about understanding how the world works and it can often be helpful to us. When the issue comes down to values, however, science cannot help any more. That is for the community to decide.

Similarly, in a trial, jury members listen carefully to the witnesses, including the expert witnesses. Once they have heard all the testimony, however, the jury retires to the jury room to make a decision on behalf of the community. A guard stands outside the room with a gun to make sure that neither the expert witnesses nor anyone else interferes with the jury.

Government: regulators, legislators, and candidates

The government could have done its job in the first place and made this whole campaign unnecessary. Instead, it circles overhead like a carrion bird, waiting for a chance to take the initiative away from your campaign.

When it sees a chance, it may use language much like that of the company's public relations staff: "We thank the fenceline neighbors group for calling everyone's attention to this problem. You were right, and we are acting accordingly, doing just what you want."

The next few sentences depend on what kind of government official is intervening:

- A regulator, such as an official from the state EPA or Department of Environmental Quality, or a representative of the state Attorney General's office, will announce they are filing legal papers of some sort. They make it clear that since the problem is in good hands now, the neighbors should stop what they are doing and go back to their daily lives.

- A sitting legislator will announce that they are preparing to intro-duce legislation to solve the problem. They will urge the neighbors to stop what they are doing and spend their time lobbying for the legislation.

- A candidate (a would-be government official) will announce that they will introduce legislation if elected. They will invite the neigh-bors to stop what they are doing and spend their time campaigning for their election.

It is tough to keep a clear head when it seems like reinforcements have just shown up to save you from being overrun by the company.

Nevertheless, you have to remember the sequence of events. Before your campaign started, the government could not have cared less about what the pollution was doing to you and your family. It did nothing to follow-up on complaints. It rubber-stamped pollution permits. It did no real air and water monitoring or health studies. Only your hard work cre-ated enough heat that the government showed up.

Guess what will happen if you suspend the campaign to see if the officials carry out their promises, or if you turn the campaign into a cheerleading squad for a legislator or candidate? No more campaign means no more heat, and that means the government officials will wander off. Worse, they will cut a bad deal with the company and then wander off.

That is not the kind of ending your campaign deserves.

A good neighbor campaign can sometimes unintentionally open the door for the government to take the initiative by centering its demands on what the government should do, rather than on what the company should do.

Appealing to the government is seldom as effective as the direct approach. Let's say your children are watching *Jerry Springer* on television and you don't like it. You could write a letter to your Congress member urging legislation. Maybe they act accordingly. Maybe it passes. Maybe the other house passes it. Maybe the President signs it. Maybe the program gets funded. Maybe the agency considers it a priority. Maybe the bureaucrats do not bungle it. Maybe the networks comply by coding their programs. Maybe electronic firms produce the blocking device for your television set. Maybe you can afford it and get around to installing it. Or, you can take the initiative and tell your children, "Turn that crap off now."

When the campaign is focused on asking the government to solve the problem, over time it can start to be more about the process than about the original goal. When a procedural hurdle is cleared after months or years—maybe a bill was voted out of committee—it is tempting to call it a victory. It is not really a victory, though, because in the community not one person's daily life has been improved. At this point, the campaign is wide open for the government to steal the initiative.

Lawyers

At some times in your campaign, no one else but a lawyer can help. If you meet a good lawyer, hang on to their phone number.

The wrong circumstances and the wrong lawyer, however, can rob you of the initiative in a hurry. Your campaign is making good progress, and a lawyer shows up to tease everyone with the possibility of riches from a lawsuit. The neighbors group cannot resist and signs up for the lawsuit, and then the lawyer starts telling them what they need to do to maximize their chances of a big payday. Each piece of advice restricts the neighbors group more. "Don't make statements to the press. The judge won't like it." "Don't talk directly to the company." "Don't have that march you were planning." "I can get you more money in a settlement if you agree not to talk about the company in the future."

Before long, the attorney is running your campaign, and the campaign is slowing to a halt. What is going on in the courtroom may be interesting, but the neighbors have lost all influence over it.

Port Arthur community leader Hilton Kelley has seen lawyers at their worst:

> Many times when [the refineries] release some chemical and our state regulatory agency finds industry to be negligent, lawyers would start circling like sharks. They would sign up a bunch of people and go after the refineries. The company would pay them three million dollars, the lawyers would make off with $1.5 million, and the community has to share the other $1.5 million. Once all is said and done, each of 3,000 people in the lawsuit class might get $400.
>
> It's a money game. Industry puts money aside because they calculate that they are going to have a certain amount of problems in a year. If they do not have those problems, the money is shifted over to the following year's pot. It's a way of doing business.[2]

Sometimes a lawsuit is the best move for a neighbors' group, but be cautious. Even with a well-intentioned attorney, pursuing a lawsuit can be arduous, time-consuming, and sometimes expensive, ineffective and a campaign-killer.

---

2. Hilton Kelley (Executive Director, Community In-power and Development Association), interview with author, May 10, 2005.

3. Taking the initiative back

Let's go back to the sports analogy, in this case, a football game. We have all seen this movie. If a team has lost the momentum, what does the coach say to them in the locker room at half time?

"We're one big play away from getting the momentum back."

And then, at the end of the pep talk, the coach prowls up and down the locker room, looking into the eyes of his players, and barking, "Who's going to make the big play to turn this game around? Is it you? Is it you? How about you?"

I do not recommend barking, but this example is a reminder that you can get the momentum back quite quickly. It just takes one big play.

Usually two steps precede the big play.

The first step is to stop reacting. By definition, when others have the initiative, they are taking the actions that move events forward, and you are reacting to what they do. You spend all your time trying to figure out how to react to the last thing they did. By the time you carry out your reaction, the people with the initiative have done something else you have to figure out how to react to. It chews up all your time and energy, and your campaign plan goes on the back burner.

For example, let's say the company has announced a Community Advisory Panel to co-opt your campaign. You could devote all your time to discussing what to do about it. Will they invite us to be on it? Who else is being invited? If invited, should we accept? Should we be on as a group, or as individuals? Should we denounce it publicly? What is the agenda? Can we affect the agenda? The questions go on and on, and they are all reactive.

Try this: Stop discussing the new panel. Just stop for a while. Now you have some time to figure out how to get your campaign back on track.

The second step is to broaden the circle of people working on the problem. Find a few people who are not as frustrated as you are because they have not been as involved as you. In the middle of explaining it to one of them, the answer may pop into your head. Or, they may say, "I know this is a stupid question, but why don't you...?" And what they suggest is something that never occurred to you. Or they may call you back the next day with three fresh ideas, having spent the evening mulling it over.

However it happens, people appreciate being asked for advice. It shows you respect them. They often return the favor with great ideas.

There is no shame in stopping to ask for directions. Consider the following example concerning Cesar Chavez and the United Farm Workers union, as described by Tom Hayden:

> The solution [to frustration] is to find a creative act that will turn the tables and get things going again. Creativity is the answer to frustration, and is a very important organizational principle.
>
> It doesn't have to be individual creativity. You don't have to go off and try to think up the answer. Often the answer comes from the people.
>
> When things were at a most frustrating point in the United Farm Worker's history, like when the big strikes were going on and on and on, Cesar at one point went to a mass meeting and said, "I know you're frustrated, you want to change direction, but ideas come from people. I know that if I was down there instead of up here, I would try to think of an idea to get us through this situation."
>
> Sure enough, three women who were just loyal pickets and had never really opened their mouths came to him a couple of hours later and said, "You wanted ideas. We're not challenging your leadership." He thought they wanted something. The problem in this case was in dealing with workers who were inside the ranch, who never had to come out. Trying to go in to meet the workers, you'd get busted, beaten, and off to jail. So the women said, "What about having an altar in a car outside the gate and having a vigil." He said, "That's it. There's more than one way to skin a cat, backwards and forwards. You can't go in so we have to get them to come out." They started a vigil and succeeded. All the farm workers came out.[3]

And the farm workers union had just regained the initiative.

---

3. Tom Hayden, *Universal patterns*, workshop, September 26, 1976, La Paz, California.

CHAPTER 5

▼

RECRUITMENT

John O'Connor

*The following was written for the pioneering 1990 book, "Fighting Toxics."
You will need to make your own decisions about, for example, whether to
charge membership dues or form a coalition. In addition, your time may be
more limited than the suggested schedule requires. Either way, in reading this
chapter, you can't help appreciating and learning from O'Connor's spirit and
discipline.—Ed.*

Cesar Chavez, the community and labor organizer who is now president of the United Farm Workers, was once asked by an aspiring young organizer, "How do you organize?"

He said, "First, you talk to one person, face to face, then you talk to another..."

"But, Cesar," the impatient youth interrupted, "how do you really get them involved?"

Chavez replied, "First, you talk to one person, face to face, and then you talk to the next and then the next..." [1]

The point is that there is no substitute, whether it's neighborhood or coalition organizing, for clear, concise, person-to-person talk. Whether it's doorknocking in the neighborhood or meeting with the parish priest or rabbi, the only way to begin is with personal conversations. There are three common approaches to recruiting members, volunteers, or coalition partners: doorknocking, house meetings, and institutional visits.

1. Doorknocking

Step One. Select your target area. Get a map of the general area and drive or walk through the neighborhood to figure out which homes are closest to the toxic site. Common sense tells you that those most concerned about cleaning up or preventing toxic emissions are the ones living closest to the problem.

Step Two. Prepare your clipboard. Its basic ingredients will include: petitions or contact sheets with space for name, address, and (especially) phone number; membership cards; a letter of reference signed by community leaders that introduces the organization and adds legitimacy; fact

---

Excerpted from *Fighting Toxics* by Gary Cohen and John O'Connor, eds. Copyright © 1990 National Toxics Campaign. Reproduced by permission of Island Press, Washington, D.C.

1. Cesar Chavez (1927–1993) founded and led the first successful farm workers' union in U.S. history, the United Farm Workers of America, AFL-CIO.—Ed.

sheets about the problem and organization; and a few news clips about your organization's work.

Step Three. Prepare yourself mentally. Doorknocking is like climbing a big hill. When you're at the bottom looking up you ask yourself. "Do I really want to climb it today? Maybe I'll put it off until tomorrow." But when you start to climb you feel invigorated, and by the time you reach the top you realize it wasn't that hard. In fact, it was good for your health. Similarly, knocking on that first door can be a scary experience. What if they slam the door in my face? What if they're not interested? But as you get going you realize what a pleasure it is to meet new, concerned people. Not only will most people be interested, but most will also sign your toxics petition and a good percentage will join your organization. As it progresses you realize that the hard work is rewarding. You develop new skills and learn from the people you meet. Remember: If you don't get out there and recruit you'll never have enough fellow citizens organized to win the dumpsite cleanup and protect children from the horrors of uncontrolled toxic substances.

Step Four. You've got your map, the clipboard is ready, you're ready, you approach that first door—but what do you say? First, introduce yourself and the name of your organization. Then you must establish credibility by legitimizing your group. Next, you have to engage the neighbor in conversation to ask what he knows or feels about the issue. If he is not talkative, describe the problem and get his opinions and concerns. Then point out the solution and give him the opportunity to take the path of action necessary to put the solution into practice. You must be able to overcome negative thinking and pessimism. You must know when to be low key and when to be fiery. There is no set formula on what to say or how to say it. Each doorknocker has to develop his or her own style, delivery, and membership appeal.

Having said this, I will nevertheless suggest one approach I developed with community organizer Mike Bishop, an approach that has been used successfully in many communities across the country. This approach, called the "five-point rap," contains the key elements that need to be covered when you're trying to recruit members, enlist volunteers, or persuade people to turn out for an upcoming event. The five points are (1) identification (name and organization), (2) legitimize your organization, (3) engage and educate, (4) membership, and (5) next event or meeting.

Obviously, the first two points are crucial when the neighbor's initial thought is, "Who is this person and why is she here?" Very quickly, you cover these points, as explained in the following paragraphs.

Point 1: Identification

"Hi, my name is Lisa Hopkins, and I'm with FIST—Families Involved in Stopping Toxics."

Point 2: Legitimize Your Organization

"You've probably heard of us. We're the organization of residents who are fighting that toxic dump that's poisoning our air and water."

At this point, it's a good idea to show the neighbor the news clips of your organization's work. Don't hand the news clip to the person since it will distract him or her from talking with you. If you hand them the clip, some people's response is to read it (or pretend to do so while they figure out a way to throw you off their doorstep).

Point 3: Engage and Educate

"We are going through the neighborhood today to see what people think we should do to get the toxic dump down the street cleaned up. Do you have any ideas about the situation, or do you think we should be working on other issues that are of concern to you?"

Resident: "No, I just know what I read in the paper, and it wasn't much!"

Don't lose them. Use careful questioning to get your neighbor talking. If people are lectured, rather than being engaged in conversation, they are less likely to get involved. When people give their opinions they feel a sense of participation in the discussion and will be more open to joining the fight than if you just talk at them. Real conversation requires two parties. Ask them what they know about past dumping. Have they smelled the toxics or tasted them in the water? Such questions engage their participation. If you ask people questions and listen to their ideas, they feel that what they say matters. Your goal as an organizer is to leave each resident with the thought that he or she is important to the organization and the neighborhood's future.

Often the people will not have a lot to say, for many reasons, so it's important to give them more facts about the problem and the ways to solve it. That's the educational side to Point 3.

Doorknocker: "Well, the main reason you don't know what is in the water is because the polluter and the government have refused to give us information about what is in the water. FIST believes that we have the right to know what toxics are in our water and how the stuff affects our health. We know from some of our research committee's work that at the very least benzene and lead are at the site. We know that benzene causes leukemia—a form of cancer. Lead can cause learning disabilities in young children. We also know that the waste is less than a mile from the town's drinking water source. We have a petition we plan to present to the government and the polluters to test our water and get us an alternative supply if it proves to be toxic. Would you look it over and sign if you think it's appropriate?"

Resident: "Well, let's see it. But tell me what you really want."

Doorknocker: "Well, first we want your signature to win the proper testing and cleanup. As you probably know, the more signatures we get, the better our chances of getting these things checked out."

Resident: "Well, okay, I'll sign, but I don't give out my phone number, you know."

Doorknocker: "Your phone number will not be given out, and will only be used to get back to you about important organizational business—like a meeting to get the water tested or something important regarding the neighborhood's health and safety."

Resident: "All right, then…here."

Point 4: Membership.

Membership is the most important part of the entire conversation. Every person approached must be given an opportunity to improve his or her life. All must be given a straightforward membership appeal—an opportunity through collective action to protect their health and safety against toxic hazards. If you don't inform people of the importance of membership at the first interview, they usually say, "I knew there was a catch to this," when the question is brought up later.

Membership is an important way to guarantee participation and turn-out. Experienced neighborhood leaders and organizers will tell you that neighborhood meetings are more fully attended right after an intensive membership drive. People who join often say to themselves, "Of course, I'm going to the meeting—I'm a member! I own a piece of the rock and I'm going to find out more about the toxic dump and what we can do." The greater the number of members that sign up and pay dues, the greater your organizational results will be.

Why is it important to pay dues as a member? First, it costs money to wage campaigns. You need money for leaflets, literature, travel, phones, postage, copying, and, if your organization gets big enough, for paid staff and office space. Corporations generally don't give to community organizing projects, especially if the company in question dumped chemicals at the site. Even if they were available, corporate funds usually come with such strings attached that the group would not be able to take the hard-hitting actions that are necessary to prevent toxic hazards.

The membership appeal must be done with ease and comfort. You must look the potential member in the eye, smile, and ask him to join. If you seem uneasy about asking, people won't join. Back to the sample appeal:

Doorknocker: "As you probably know (nodding your head), our organization, like every other organization, needs money to accomplish our toxic cleanup campaign. Not much, but some. That's why we are on a membership drive. Membership is only $25 a year; that's less than $3 per month—less than the cost of a six-pack these days. The big issue is not the money, but rather the power that we have to improve the situation. The more dues-paying members we have, the better our chances of getting the toxic dump cleaned up. Would you like to become a member?"

Resident: "Sure, I'll join."

(Hand him the card or the membership form to fill out.)

Point 5: Next Event or Meeting.

What if your neighbor says, "No, I don't know enough about it yet."

Doorknocker: "Well, then come to the next meeting this month and see what good work we're doing. Once you see us in action, I'm sure you'll want to join. Here's a flyer about the meeting that will be held at St. James Church, two weeks from tonight, June 1st at 7:30 PM. Thanks for your time. Nice talking with you."

Too often, people make the mistake of telling the resident about the next big meeting or event before the membership appeal. The familiar response is, "Oh, I'll come to the meeting and then decide if I'll join." Membership, however, is the best guarantee of getting someone to attend the meeting, action, or event. People follow their money!

2. House meetings

House meetings are another way to build your local toxics organization. Before you hold a big organizational event, organize several smaller meeting in members' apartments or homes. The host family can invite friends, neighbors, and relatives who might become active in the organization. Apart from recruiting, house meetings are a good way of developing the skills of new members. Often when new members enter an organization, there is not enough opportunity for them to take on the roles that challenge, develop and test new leaders. Taking a leadership role in house meetings is the first step to developing the skills necessary to run meetings, plan actions, and build the organization.

The house-meeting format is straightforward. The host welcomes everyone and introduces people to each other. Then someone (not necessarily the host) explains what the organization is, its goals and objectives, and how the group works. A new member who wants to take on a leadership role can give this explanation. House meetings give people practice in understanding and projecting the organization's mission. On the other hand, you may want an experienced leader to explain the organization's goals. They can project the necessary experience and confidence to recruit new members and volunteers.

3. Institutional visits and coalition building

One of the most difficult jobs in organizing is building a coalition around a common purpose. If you want to fight toxic pollution in your backyard, the first step is to build a membership organization of people living closest to the site, since they are the ones who have the greatest self-interest. Once you have built your own organization, only then should you think about working in coalition with other groups. There are only rare exceptions to this rule.

Whenever you approach an organization to join in your efforts, you must appeal to that organization's self-interest. What benefits will other groups gain by joining your toxics coalition? If the neighborhood dump is not detoxified, for example, is there a danger that toxic chemicals could permeate the neighborhood to such a degree that it would have to be evacuated, as in the case of Love Canal? If you're trying to get a synagogue to join your coalition and the problem is as bad as Love Canal or Times Beach, you could suggest to the rabbi that there might not be a synagogue anymore if this toxic problem is not remedied.[2] Always appeal to people's self-interest.

Here are some key questions to ask before approaching other organizations:

> What power would other groups bring to the coalition?
> What problems would other groups bring to the coalition?
> What does your group stand to lose by working in a coalition?

---

2. Love Canal, New York, was built partly on 21,000 tons of toxic waste, including chlorobenzene, dioxin, halogenated organics, and pesticides. After neighbors noticed odors and residues from seeping wastes, and high levels of birth defects and other illnesses, thousands of people had to relocate. In 1982, health problems began to be reported in Times Beach, Missouri, and investigators learned that a firm spraying oil on roads to control dust was, in fact, using waste oil laden with toxic chemical wastes. More than 2,000 people had to relocate.—Ed.

What is the price of the support of other organizations?
What are the issues to avoid?
Under what sort of structure will the coalition function?
What groups are potential coalition members?
How will the coalition function? Who makes decisions?

Once you've figured out the answers to these questions, it's time to start talking to people. When you approach potential coalition members, you can use a version of the five-point rap. First, introduce yourself and tell them about your organization and the coalition that's being formed. Ask them about the issues they think the coalition should be working on. Describe your goals for the coalition. Then solicit their support (as in the membership appeal in the doorknocking format).

At each visit ask your potential coalition partner to help out in some way. Always ask for the big things first. If you ask them to send a representative to sit on the coalition board for assigned staff time and they say no, they might just let you use the hall. If they say no to using the hall, they probably won't join the coalition. People basically like to help others in need. If institutional representatives are even slightly interested, put them on a mailing list and keep them informed.

In building coalitions, think what you can offer other groups you want to solicit. Bring your members to their fundraiser. Show up for their picket line. Coalition building requires good human relations. As West Coast organizer Tim Sampson says, "The flowers of organizational relations grow from personal interest, kindness, and cultivation."

Coalitions must be built locally, statewide, regionally, and then nationally to solve the country's toxic chemical crisis. But remember this central caution: Coalition attempts can be a dangerous distraction from building a powerful local membership organization. Build your neighborhood organization first.

One final note on all forms of recruitment: There is a saying that "organizations are either growing or dying." Growing depends on a permanent recruitment campaign. The lifeblood of all organizations is a constant influx of new members. All organizational power flows from the strength of its members. The more people you have, the more you can do to clean up and prevent toxic hazards.

4. General recruitment drive

The recruitment drive generally last eight weeks—and the organizers or community leaders may be working more hours in this period than in any other phase of the drive. Get ready to spend full workweeks on recruitment. In addition to working five to six hours a day knocking on doors, the remainder of your time should be slotted for institutional visits, careful record keeping of all interested contacts on 3-by-5 index cards, research, new fact sheets, and planning for the organizing committee and house meetings.

Doorknocking should lead to seven or eight good conversations per hour. Whenever possible, you should try to actually get in the door, but talking on the porch will do. Use the five-point rap described earlier. Make sure everybody signs a petition: names and phone numbers are the key pieces of information.

During the recruitment drive, ask everybody to join and get people talking. Remember, you're looking for potential leaders who are not only articulate but also have a base of supporters through their affiliations and also have some time and willingness to work. In the first four weeks, recruitment should consist of "cold" doorknocking in the late afternoon until evening. Generally, 3:00 PM to 9:00 PM are acceptable hours. Retirement communities can be canvassed earlier in the day. Saturdays and Sundays are also available—lots of people are home then. Keep careful records of homes that don't answer and go back at other times—some of the best leaders may not be home when you first show up. By the tail end of the fourth week and beginning of the fifth week, you can do home visits to set up house meetings and the first organizing committee meeting.

By the fifth week, home visits begin to replace a couple of hours of the cold doorknocking each day. Your purpose is to see if these people will agree either to sit on the organizing committee (if you think they're leadership material) or to hold a house meeting. Take time to find out what makes people tick. Are they part of a church or other organization? Who else do they know that might be interested in joining the local campaign?

House meetings serve two purposes: to recruit new people to the organizing process and to test leaders who might have potential—can they turn out their friends and neighbors and help orchestrate the meeting? There should be at least four house meetings as part of the drive from weeks five through eight. A typical agenda includes introductions, discussion of issues, explanation of the organization, collection of dues, and recruitment strategies.

CHAPTER 6

▼

CRIME SCENE
INVESTIGATION:
TOOLS YOU CAN USE TO
CATCH AND EXPOSE
POLLUTION

Denny Larson

Global Community Monitor is a nonprofit organization based in San Francisco. We work all over the world with people who are breathing odors and particles, from landfills and refineries to steel, chemical and pharmaceutical plants. They want to find out one simple thing: What am I breathing?

In most cases, nobody can answer them, because the air is not being monitored in the hot spot where they live. The agency says, "We've got a network of monitors, and we're checking them regularly, and the plant is in compliance."

Then the fenceline neighbors figure out that the monitors are in the wrong place checking for the wrong chemicals at the wrong time. The existing system gives the company and the government the answer they want—that there's no problem—so they don't have to do anything about it.

But there really is a problem.

Many of the gas clouds, particle snowstorms and odors are not a routine part of the operation. It happens too much; it is called "upset pollution." It is caused by something a little bit wrong in the process. Maybe they don't have the right equipment to prevent it, or maybe they're running over capacity.

Where we've studied this with particular industries like oil refining, we've found that the emissions released in a single hour-long upset event can exceed the yearly reported emissions of a facility. Many of these plants have upsets all the time. Regardless of what happens, the company will say that no chemicals were released: "We tested. We found nothing. The levels were safe."

When we look at industrial pollution, we tend to think first about what's coming out of the smokestacks. However, what is leaking out of the pipes and the tanks, called "fugitive emissions," are often two to five times higher than smokestack emissions. The upsets, spills and incidents can total six to ten times higher than the yearly reported emissions.

Bucket brigades

The "bucket" is an inexpensive air monitoring device, which is both homemade and U.S. EPA-certified. The bucket brigade is a metaphor for what we're doing. If you remember your history lessons, when there was a fire in the old pioneer town, everybody got together and formed a line between the creek and the burning house. Working as a team, they passed buckets of water and they put out the fire.

Modern-day bucket brigades work the same way, as a team, staying in touch with one another about what's happening with these odors and pollution, and documenting the facts consistently.

If you are a neighbor of a polluting factory, you are a witness to an environmental crime in progress. You need to turn hearsay or anecdotal "talk on the street" into hard, clear, cold evidence. If you want to solve a crime, that's what it's about, as you know if you watch any of the CSI shows on television. This is just a community toxic crime.

To start, we look at the kinds of pollution the company itself says the plant puts out. As a bucket brigade member, you would test for that and document it. For example, you would determine whether you are downwind of it when it occurs, in the impact zone. You would fill out evidentiary sheets, which are essentially affidavits. You would swear that you were standing here and the wind was blowing from the plant toward your neighborhood and it started snowing soot and you tested it. Let's say the plant reports that it puts out barium, copper and mercury. You test the air, and when the test results get back, guess what was in the air sample? Barium, copper and mercury. It fits together.

The Bucket Brigade is not a scientific experiment. Our focus is on organizing. We use science, but only in the service of organizing. How do you achieve power with a giant company out there? You've got to be organized. You've got to bring more people in and use that as a way to work together.

Global Community Monitor doesn't come in with an agenda, telling you what should be done in your neighborhood or city. We give you advice and tools, and you're the ones who are going to decide what is happening and what needs to happen with the company.

A Bucket Brigade uses a set of tools from a simple pollution log all the way up to doing complicated testing yourself.

From a practical standpoint, you can't give everybody a bucket and take a test every day. The tests are fairly expensive for one thing. There's a way, though, for everyone to participate in a bucket brigade to feed into that.

Logbooks

The first tool is a logbook. These are a simple-looking but powerful way to record key pieces of information systematically over time.

When a soot snowstorm is happening in your back yard or you're getting hit at 11:00 PM by an odor, go to your log sheets and write that down. What is it? When did it start? How long did it go on? Maybe it started at 11:00 PM and went until 2:00 AM. It's important that you note the wind direction, because in many places, there are many possible pollution sources out there. The wind direction is evidence of where it came from. What did you see? Did you see a big flare? Was a cloud coming out of the plant? Were there loud sounds? Did you hear the roaring of pressure being let off?

Be descriptive about what you smell. Sometimes people find this hard to do. Some smells are easy to identify, like the rotten-egg smell. Other chemicals have known odors as well. There's such a thing as odor science, and dozens of research papers have documented that specific chemicals have specific odors. For example, Mercaptan sulfur compounds smell like rotten cabbage. Being descriptive about the specific odors is going to help get to the bottom of what they are.

Neighbors should get together and agree among themselves what those particular smells are. Put a name on it, agree on it, and there will be more consistency when you are doing your log sheets.

Fenceline neighbors in the SIPCOT Industrial Area, Cuddalore, India, came up with the following list of chemical smells:[1]

---

1. SIPCOT Area Community Environmental Monitor, http://
   www.sipcotcuddalore.com.

Acid

Ammonia

Burning plastic or electric cable

Burnt body/Corpse burning

Burnt curry/Burnt gravy

Burnt material

Burnt rice

Burnt rubber

Chikoo fruit

Chilli powder

Crushed neem seed/cake/oil

Decaying corpse/Dead body

Dead animal

Dough roasted and grounded

Firecracker

Fruit juice

Ground bone

Hospital

Human excreta

Kerosene

Mosquito coil

Nail paint

Paint

Phenyl

Public toilet

Roasted sugar

Rotten eggs

Rotten fruits

Rotten jackfruit

Rotten milk

Sewer/gutter smell

Sour

Sulphur

Sweet and sugarcane like

Spirit/alcohol smell

Urine smell

Neighbors in the Tremont community in Cleveland, Ohio, next to the giant Mittal Steel complex, report the following smells:

Rotten eggs

Boiled eggs

Burning toast

Sweet chemical

Rotting fruit

Asphalt

Vomit

Nail polish

Melting plastic or crayon

Garlic

Companies or government agencies often say that it's just an odor; it might smell bad, but it won't harm you.

Recent research compared how much of various chemicals it took for the human nose to smell them with how much was a health danger.[2] For sulfur dioxide, the odor threshold is 1220, the danger threshold is 80.[3] That means that by the time you can smell it, the concentration is already 15 times higher than the health danger level. It is not just an odor.

Like poison, toxic chemicals target certain organs of the body. Some chemicals attack your eyes. Others attack the brain. Others attack the cardiovascular system. We're working with a pulp mill in Humboldt County, California, and many people there are having eye problems that can be caused by the sulfur it puts out.

If you look up a chart of toxic chemicals in an occupational health manual, one column is labeled "target organs." It means that when the chemical enters your body, it disrupts that organ or bodily function.

Buckets

A bucket brigade tests the neighborhood air using an ordinary hardware store bucket, with a few changes.

The bucket is a mechanical lung. When you're breathing chemicals that make you feel bad, taking an air sample is like making this mechanical lung breathe in at the same time you do. Unlike your lungs, we can ship this to the laboratory and test what's in it.

If they monitor at all, companies and agencies usually use a Summa canister, which costs about a thousand dollars. It is lined with stainless steel or glass, and vacuum-sealed. It sucks the air in, you connect it to a gas

---

2. R.E.Ruthenberg, "Odor perception thresholds versus danger levels of airborne gases and particulate matter," (September 18, 2002), http://www.sipcotcuddalore.com/odor_threshold_report.html.

3. The units are micrograms/cubic meter. Converting this to parts per million (ppm) or parts per billion (ppb) requires a different conversion factor for each chemical based on its molecular weight. The important number in this example is the 15/1 ratio, which is the same regardless of the units used.

chromatograph, and a fancy computer tells you what chemicals are in there.

We couldn't use a Summa canister because so many neighborhoods need air-sampling devices, and they couldn't afford a thousand-dollar piece of equipment. We needed to find or invent something a lot cheaper, a poor man's Summa canister. You can build an EPA-certified bucket for $125, including an industry-standard $15 Tedlar sampling bag that does not react to gases or give off its own gases. The lab fees are $515 a sample for the complete range of tests for 89 chemicals and sulfur compounds, but if we target just the chemicals that your target plant puts out, the cost is much less.

There's no substitute for hands-on training, but here is a quick summary of how a bucket works.

The bucket has a little nose connected to the lung (sampling bag). A little pressure fitting holds the bag in place. The air is going to come through the nose and fill the lung up. On the other side are a hole and a hose.

You may remember the vacuum principle from physics class because it is keeping you alive right now. That's how your lungs operate. The muscles connected to your diaphragm are pulling your lungs open and closed. Nothing is pumping air down your nose. Your diaphragm is pulling your lungs open; that's why you're breathing right now.

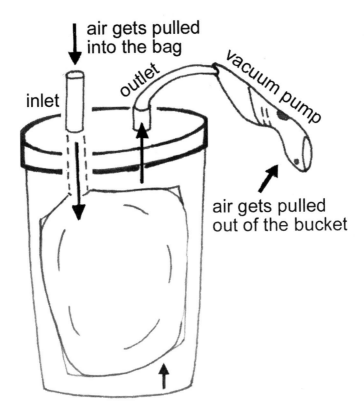

air gets pulled into the bag

inlet

outlet

vacuum pump

air gets pulled out of the bucket

The bucket doesn't have a diaphragm, but it does have a pump to create the same pressure. If you pumped air in to the bucket, that would just give you a sample of pump air, and you're probably not interested in the components of plastic pump air. You're interested in the stench coming into the neighborhood. To do that, you pump air *out* of the bucket, creating vacuum pressure inside, and it's going to pull the bag open.

The bag has a valve on it so you can make sure that air isn't leaking into it for two or three weeks before you take the sample. You open the bag's valve right before you collect a sample.

Next, crank the pump on, and it sucks air out of the bucket through the hole and the hose. The nose cap is still on, so the bucket can't breathe in yet. Inside the bucket enough negative pressure is building up in there so that it can pull the bag open. After a half-minute, pop open the nose and keep the pump running for two or three minutes more. During this time, air is flowing in through the nose and filling that bag with a grab-sample of air.

After the sampling period, close the nose, turn off the pump, open up the bucket, close the valve on the bag, disconnect the bag, and you're done.

Good accurate samples

The sampling should be as accurate as possible, grabbing that particular odor or odors people are complaining about, and getting it in that bag in the cleanest possible way without cross contamination.

For example, let's say you are at a street corner and the wind is coming toward you from the plant. In between you and the plant, however, is a busy road. Take the bucket and walk across the street so that you are upwind from the cars. You do that because you want to test the plant emissions, not car exhaust. You don't want to cross-contaminate it. That's an example of the fifty-dollar term "quality assurance quality control." It just means be smart about what you're doing. If something is in between the bucket and the gases, get it out of the way if you can.

These gases are just floating by through the air, so when you try to grab it and get it into a sample bag, it's got to be done right. It is a learned experience, like riding a bike. You have to judge the strength of the odor. The best time to take your sample is when the odor is strong. You rely on your experience to tell you, "This smells worse than this," or "This is a light odor." When you are out on a pollution patrol with the bucket, ask one another, "On a scale of one-to-ten, is that a one or is that a ten? Or somewhere in between?" We want to sample at the 7, 8, 9, and 10 levels. Ask one another, "Which odor is that? Is it a rotten-egg odor or a burnt-toast odor or what?" Ask if it is the target plant's particular odor, and you can identify it. You don't want to sample random odors, just the ones coming from your target facility.

At the lab

Then you send the bag to the laboratory, where they have a library of chemical fingerprints.

The method uses the same method astronomers use to figure out what a star is made up of. When they shoot light through various gases, each gives off a unique spectrum of colors, a fingerprint.

When your sample bag arrives, the lab technicians shoot a light beam through the air sample. The spectrum wavelengths or fingerprints will come up on their computer screen, and they'll compare it to the library. Maybe they'll check for benzene and it matches. Then they'll be able to say they found benzene in the sample. Then they will quantify it, so they can say there were 500 parts per billion of benzene, or whatever.

Two weeks after you take the sample, the lab report comes back and you find out which of 89 different gases were in the air sample.

Then you can compare the results to health-based standards, if there are any health-based standards for what you are breathing. In Norco, Louisiana, next to the chemical plant, neighbors were breathing twenty different chemicals with every single breath. Some of the levels of those chemicals were way above anything considered safe. When the agencies set a "safe" level for benzene or any other chemical, they don't consider the nineteen other chemicals you may be breathing. They don't set a standard for a safe level of more than one chemical at a time going into your lungs. So there are limitations to these health-based levels. Remember one thing: breathing these chemicals has never been proved to be "good" for you.

Chain of custody

Just like when police detectives gather evidence, you'll need to fill out a "chain of custody" record every time you take a sample. When the police come and take a blood sample from a crime scene, they have to fill out a chain of custody form, which essentially becomes an affidavit. In it, they swear that they went to such-and-such corner to investigate a shooting, and gathered this blood sample at this time on this date and here were the circumstances.

Our chain of custody form serves the same purpose, accompanies the sample to the laboratory, and becomes part of the hard evidence.

A classic example of a broken chain of custody was in the O.J. Simpson case. When the chain of custody form was examined, it documented that blood samples were collected from the scene of the crime, a policeman took them to the lab, and the lab technician signed that he'd received it, and so on. There was a gap of seven or eight hours on the form, however, in which there was no accounting for who had custody of the samples. The defense used that gap to drive a truck through the murder claims.

In filling out the chain of custody, it's important that you record date, time, place and conditions.

What makes the chain of custody work, however, is at the bottom. There are a series of signature lines, starting with the person who takes the sample. Every person that sample is passed to has to sign that they took possession of it, and when. The chain of custody has to be unbroken.

Let's say a neighbor takes a sample, and calls a friend to pick it up and drive it to FedEx. She'll sign the first line saying she gave up the sample at 4 PM on November 29, and her friend will immediately sign that he received the sample at 4 PM on November 29. The chain is not broken. And when the friend gets to the FedEx office, and he's ready to turn it over for shipping to the lab, he signs that he gave up that sample to the FedEx worker at 5 pm on November 29, and he will ask the FedEx worker to sign that they received it at that time.

On the analysis side of the form, you write what chemicals you want the lab to test for, for example, the full suite of volatile organic compounds and sulfurs. This can only be determined case-by-case in consultation with people experienced in air monitoring, but we target the known emissions from the facility.

On the right side of the form is space for comments. What's on the log sheet is what goes here. What did you experience? What did you see? What did you hear? What did you smell? What did the odor smell like? Did you have any health effects? Was it a rotten egg odor that caused you to have a stomachache? From what direction was the wind blowing?

These forms must go with the sample to the lab. You could make yourself a copy before you send it off, or get multiple sheet carbon-paper forms from the lab so you can just separate.

"We're in compliance"

The company you're dealing with will say it's in compliance. Are they?

When you are speeding down the highway, your compliance is measured with a radar gun. If you take the radar gun away from the cop, you can speed at 1,000 mph, then go to court and say, "Judge, I was in compliance." You're going to get away with it because you know nobody's got any data on you.

In our neighborhoods, we can cut through all that, saying, "You know what, we have our own radar guns right now. We're going to turn them on and see if you're in compliance or not. We are not going to wait for local or state agencies to test. We're going to do it ourselves. If the company or the government agencies want to challenge that, then bring 'em on. Get them out here with the right kind of testing equipment at the right time and the right place. We'll see who's in compliance and who isn't."

For much of what the companies are discharging, however, there isn't a legal standard of what can be in the air in your neighborhood, so any amount is legal. You can still say, "Let's say you're in compliance with the law, you're not in compliance with me living here. I can't stand the stink. I'm not going to take this pollution raining down on me any more. Here's my compliance standard for your company and you're going to meet that."

At the end of the day, you are living here, so you should set your own community standard.

The beauty of good neighbor campaigns is that each community determines what the community standard should be. The community standard in the Tremont and Slavic Village neighborhoods in Cleveland might be different than in Addyston, Ohio, where the Lanxess chemical plant is. It's up to the community to decide what they are willing to breathe, how much stink they are going to put up with, and how much they want the company to invest to clean up its act. And the community can decide for itself how much they want the company to do more monitoring so they can find out what it is coming across the fenceline.

The people in these neighborhoods know exactly what's going on

Using the bucket in community organizing campaigns trains people in a community to understand air pollution. They take their own samples and get ownership that way.

This is a totally different approach from the way some big organizations operate. Right now we're working with our sister groups in Texas and Louisiana to do environmental monitoring around the Katrina and Rita hurricane disasters. We're involving the community in the design of those tests. They are participating in gathering the samples if they want to, and they're getting to see the data first before it is broadcast to the media. They are also deciding how to use that data.

Other groups have flown in scientists, who scurry around taking tests, never talking to the neighbors, and releasing the data before they even tell the neighbors what's in their neighborhood. At the end of the day, the communities get nothing out of that. They don't understand the experience. It is treating people like they're part of an experiment, which is not right.

We have a different model of doing things. It may be faster the other way. Global Community Monitor could do more tests if we parachuted in and did it ourselves. It just wouldn't come out as well, though, because I wouldn't be incorporating all the knowledge the community has. I wouldn't know it without hearing from the neighbors: What are the odors specific to each plant? How strong is this odor compared to how bad it gets? People in the neighborhood have a lifetime of specific knowledge about the problem in their heads.

Using the buckets confirms and validates the community's experience. These companies and agency officials are totally devaluing that valuable knowledge. The people in these neighborhoods know exactly what's going on. They know what happens, when it happens, what part of the plant it's coming from, and what the harm is. They know a lot, and if the people at the company and the agencies would just pay attention to them, they could solve the problem.

Instead, they spend their money on public relations, smiling and charming the pants off you. That's costly. Then they run ads, and go through the neighborhood offering to buy playground equipment for the school, and put a sign on it, "Courtesy of blah-blah-blah corporation." They do that in direct response to people complaining about pollution. It's a good thing to buy playground equipment and support community development projects. It's not a good thing to do that when what people are complaining about is pollution and their health. They want a solution to that.

We work with neighbors of Shell Oil all over the world. Shell has a department full of people called "reputation managers." The head of this department reports directly to the CEO. The reputation managers evaluate, for example, negative newspaper articles on their pollution problems and community group campaigns. They calculate the economic cost of an article to the company's image. They come up with a dollar figure, and recommend to the CEO how much money in advertising, public relations, playground equipment and community projects it will take to whitewash it over. It's an economic equation.

It may seem like they don't care about their reputation. They may seem like notorious polluters who don't care about anything. They are also businessmen, however, and they value and invest in their reputation. The reputation managers are reporting that the neighbors have cost the company this much so far, and they're just getting started. They'll project that if the neighbors keep going, this is what it's going to cost the company. At some point, they say, "How much is it going to cost to make these guys go away?"

That's when you get down to brass tacks with them. You find yourself at the table with them, which is where you want to be as neighbors. You don't want the state agency there negotiating on your behalf. You are the people who should be negotiating about what it takes to make this a better place to live. You are the ones at the end of the day who are going to stay here and live with the results, not the plant manager or regulator or even the staff of an environmental group.

Pollution log

This is a model pollution log. When you make your own, substitute your own local pollution sights and local odors. Once these reports are filled in, collect them and turn them into reports.

Please use this log to record pollution you experience in your neighborhood or at home.

Name_____

Street_____

City, State, Zip_____

Phone_____Email_____

Date_____Time started_____Time Ended_____

Source_____

Wind direction_____

I see:

Smoke □ Flare □ Toxic cloud □ Fire □ Explosion □ Dust □

Please describe

I smell:

Rotten eggs □ Gasoline □ Heavy oil □ Sweet □ Sour □ Bitter □ Other □

Please describe_____

I feel:

Burning eyes ☐ Nose/throat irritation ☐ Breathing problem ☐ Skin irritation ☐ Other ☐

Please describe_____

To register a complaint about air pollution, call—

For more information, call—

CHAPTER 7

▼

THE TEN MOST IMPORTANT THINGS YOU CAN KNOW ABOUT FUNDRAISING

Kim Klein

Many times at the end of a training or a speech about fundraising techniques and principles, I am asked, "What are the most important things to remember?" Usually the person asking is either a volunteer with little time to help with fundraising, a person new to fundraising and overwhelmed by the number of details she or he has to keep in mind, or a staff person who is not responsible for fundraising but wants to help.

Over the years, I have thought about what I consider the ten most important things to know about fundraising. The items are not presented in order of importance, although #1 is probably the most important; nor are they in order of difficulty. If there is any order, it is the order in which I understood these things and integrated them into my own fundraising work. Undoubtedly, other skilled fundraisers would have slightly different lists, but this list has served me well for many years. I hope you find it useful.

1. If you want money, you have to ask for it.

While there are some people (may their kind increase) who will simply send an organization money or offer money without being asked, there are not enough of them to build a donor base around. Most people will not think to give you money unless you make your needs known. This is not because they are cheap or self-centered; it is because most people have no idea how much it costs to run a nonprofit, or how nonprofits get money. If you don't ask them, they will simply assume you are getting the money somewhere. They have no reason to think your group needs money unless you tell them, the same way they have no reason to know if you are hungry, or unhappy, or needing advice.

Millard Fuller, who founded Habitat for Humanity, says, "I have tried raising money by asking for it, and by not asking for it. I always got more by asking for it."

Reprinted with permission from Grassroots Fundraising,
www.grassrootsfundraising.org, (888) 458-8588.

2. Thank before you bank.

Once you receive money, you must thank the person who gave it to you. I have found that disciplining myself not to deposit checks until I have written the thank-you notes has forced me to make thank-you notes a priority. I am not rigid about this rule because if I get behind in my thank-you notes, and then don't deposit the checks for a while, the donors may wonder whether we really needed the money.

Thank-you notes do not need to be fancy and should not be long. If at all possible, they should include a personal note, even if it is from someone who doesn't know the donor. You can add something as simple as, "Hope to meet you sometime," or "Check out our website," or "Happy holidays," or even, "Thanks again—your gift really helps."

Many organizations have created note cards for staff and volunteers to use when writing thank yous. The front of the card has the logo of the group, on the top half of the inside is a relevant meaningful quote from a famous person, and the bottom half of the inside is used for the thank-you message. It is a small space, so you really can't say much. Many databases will print out a thank-you note after you enter the information about the donor—saving valuable time. These are best if accompanied by a personal note at the bottom.

Late thank yous are better than no thank you at all, but photocopied form thank yous are almost the same as no thank you.

The long and the short of thank yous is: if you don't have time to thank donors, you don't have time to have donors.

3. Donors are not ATMs

A survey of donors who gave away more than $5,000 a year asked, "What is your relationship with your favorite group?" Several gave similar answers, even though they did not know each other and did not give to the same group. All the answers were on this theme: "I would love to be considered a friend, but I am more of an ATM. They come to me when they need money, they tell me how much, I give it to them, and the next time I hear from them is when they need more."

This is a terrible indictment of much of what passes as fundraising. When I have described this common situation in trainings, people have often asked, "How can we make sure our donors don't feel this way?" The answer is very simple, "Make sure you don't feel that way about your donors."

All groups have a few "high maintenance" donors, and may be forgiven for wishing them to go on a long trip to a place without phones or e-mail. But the majority of donors require practically no attention. They have the resilience of cacti—the slightest care makes them bloom. Thank-you notes, easy-to-understand newsletters, and occasional respectful requests for extra gifts will keep people giving year in and year out.

Think of your donors as ambassadors for your group. Design your materials so that donors will be proud to give your newsletter to a friend or recommend your group when their service club or professional association is looking for an interesting speaker, or forward your e-mails to several of their colleagues.

By treating your donors as whole people who have a number of gifts to offer your group, including their financial support, you will have more financial support from existing donors, more fun fundraising, more donors, and the peace of mind of knowing that you are not treating anyone as an object.

4. Most money comes from people, and most of those people are not rich.

There are three sources of funding for all the nonprofits in the United States: earned income (such as products and fees for service), government (public sector), and the private sector, which includes foundations, corporations and individuals. For the nearly 60 years that records about who gives money away have been kept, at least 80% of this money has been shown to be given by individuals.

In 2002, total giving by the private sector was almost $241 billion, and 84.2 percent of that ($202 billion) was given away by individuals! These people are all people—there is no significant difference in giving patterns by age, race, or gender. Income is not nearly the variable that one would think: middle-class, working-class and poor people are generous givers and account for a high percentage of the money given away. In fact, a study by Arthur Blocks of the Maxwell School of Citizenship and Public Affairs at Syracuse University showed that 19% of families living on welfare give away an average of $72 a year!

Too often, people think they can't raise money because they don't know any wealthy philanthropists. It is a great comfort to find that the people we know, whoever they are, are adequate to the task. Seven out of ten adults give away money. Focus your work on these givers, and help teach young people to become givers.

5. People have the right to say no.

One of the biggest mistakes I made early on as a fundraising trainer was not balancing my emphasis on the need to ask for money with the reality that people are going to say no. No one is obligated to support your group—no matter what you have done for them, no matter how wealthy they are, no matter how much they give to other groups, how close a friend they are of the director, or any other circumstance that makes it seem they would be a likely giver. While it is possible to guilt-trip, trick, or manipulate someone into giving once, that will not work as a repeat strategy. People avoid people who make them feel bad, and they are attracted to people who make them feel good. When you can make someone feel all right about saying no, you keep the door open to a future yes, or to that person referring someone else to your group.

People say no for all kinds of reasons: they don't have extra money right now; they just gave to another group; they don't give at the door, over the phone, by mail; a serious crisis in their family is consuming all their emotional energy; they are in a bad mood. Rarely does their refusal have anything to do with you or your group. Sometimes people say no because they have other priorities, or they don't understand what your group does. Sometimes we hear no when the person is just saying, "I need more time to decide," or "I need more information," or "I have misunderstood something you said."

So, first be clear that the person is saying no, and not something else like, "Not now," or "I don't like special events." Once you are certain that the person has said no, accept it. Go on to your next prospect. If appropriate, write the person a letter and thank them for the attention they gave to your request. Then let it go. If you don't hear no several times a week, you are not asking enough people.

6. To be good at fundraising, cultivate three traits.

A good fundraiser requires three character traits as much as any set of skills. These traits are first, a belief in the cause for which you are raising money and the ability to maintain that belief during defeats, tedious tasks, and financial insecurity; second, the ability to have high hopes and low expectations, allowing you to be often pleased but rarely disappointed; and third, faith in the basic goodness of people.

While fundraising is certainly a profession, people who will raise money for any kind of group are rarely effective. Fundraising is a means to an end, a way to promote a cause, a very necessary skill in achieving goals and fulfilling missions.

7. Fundraising should not be confused with fund chasing, fund squeezing, or fund hoarding.

Too often, organizations get confused about what fundraising is and is not.

If you hear that a foundation is now funding XYZ idea, and your organization has never done work in that area nor have you ever wished to do work in that area, the fact that you are well qualified to do such work is immaterial. To apply for a grant just because the money is available and not because the work will promote your mission is called fund chasing. Many groups chase money all over and, in doing so, move very far away from their mission.

Similarly, if your organization seems to be running into a deficit situation, cutting items out of the budget may be necessary but should not be confused with fundraising. When deficits loom, the fund squeezing question is, "How can we cut back on spending?"; the fundraising question is "Where can we get even more money?"

Finally, putting money aside for a rainy day, or taking money people have given you for annual operating and program work and being able to put some of it into a savings account is a good idea. Where savings becomes hoarding, however, is when no occasion seems important enough to warrant using the savings.

I know a number of groups that have cut whole staff positions and program areas rather than let money sitting in their savings be used to keep them going until more money could be raised. I know groups that overstate what they pay people, what price they pay for equipment, what they spend on rent, all to get bigger grants from foundations or larger gifts from individuals, and then put that extra into savings—savings that they have no plan for.

A group that saves money needs to have a rationale: Why are you saving this money? Under what circumstances would you spend it? Without some plan in mind, the group simply hoards money.

Fund chasing, fund squeezing, and fund hoarding need to be replaced with an ethic that directs the group to seek the money it needs, spend it wisely, and set some aside for cash-flow emergencies or future work.

8. Fundraising is an exchange—People pay you to do work they cannot do alone.

Hank Rosso, founder of the Fund Raising School and my mentor for many years, spoke often about the need to eliminate the idea that fundraising was like begging.

Begging is when you ask for something you do not deserve. If you are doing good work, then you deserve to raise the money to do it. What you must do is figure out how to articulate what you are doing so that the person hearing it, if they share your values, will want to exchange their money for your work. They will pay you to do work they cannot do alone.

9. People's anxieties about fundraising stem from their anxieties about money.

Anxiety about money is learned, and it can be unlearned. If you are ever around children, you know that they have no trouble asking for anything, especially money. In fact, if you say no to a child's request for money, they will simply ask again, or rephrase their request ("I'll only spend it on books"), or offer an alternative ("How about if I do the dishes, then will you give me the money?").

Everything we think and feel about money we have been taught. None of it is natural; none of it is genetic. In fact, in many countries around the world, people talk easily about money. They discuss what they earn, how much they paid for things, and it is not considered rude to ask others about salaries and costs.

We have been taught not to talk about money or to ask for it, except under very limited circumstances. Many of us are taught that money is a private affair. Having too little or too much can be a source of shame and embarrassment, yet money is also a source of status and power. Most people would like to have more money, yet most will also admit that money doesn't buy happiness.

As adults, we have the right—in fact, the obligation—to examine the ideas we were taught as children to ensure that they are accurate and that they promote values we want to live by as adults. Most of us have changed our thinking about sex and sexuality, about race, about age, illness and disability, about religion, about marriage, about how children should be raised, what foods are healthy, and much more. We have done this as we have learned more, as we have experienced more, or as we have thought about what we value and what we do not.

We need to take the time to do the same work with our attitudes toward money. We can choose attitudes that make sense and that promote our health and well-being.

Our attitudes toward fundraising are a subset of our larger attitudes toward money. The most important change we can make in our attitudes toward fundraising is to remember that success in fundraising is defined by how many people you ask rather than how much money you raise. This is because some people are going to say no, which has got to be all right with you. The more people you ask, the more yes answers you will eventually get.

Finally, if you are anxious about asking for money or would rather not ask, this is normal. But ask yourself if what you believe in is bigger than what you are anxious about. Keep focused on your commitment to the cause and that will propel you past your doubts, fears, and anxieties.

10. There are four steps to fundraising—plan, plan, plan, and work your plan.

Though humorous, this formula that I learned from a community organizer underscores the fact that fundraising is three parts planning for one part doing. I learned this later in my career, after having gone off half-cocked into many fundraising campaigns and programs. I meant to plan, I planned to make a plan, I just never got around to planning.

I have learned (usually the hard way) that an hour of planning can save five hours of work, leaving much more time both to plan and to work. Planning also avoids that awful feeling of "How can I ever get everything done," and that sense of impending doom. It moves us out of crisis mentality and means that we are going to be a lot easier for our co-workers to get along with.

There are a lot of articles and books on planning—I recommend reading some of them. However, the easiest way I have found to plan something is to start by defining the end result you want and when you want it to happen, then work backwards from that point to the present. For example, if you want your organization to have 100 new members by the end of next year and you are going to use house parties as your primary acquisition strategy, you will need to schedule five to seven house parties that will recruit 10 to 15 members per party.

To set up one house party will require asking three people to host it (only one will accept), which will require identifying 15 or 20 possible hosts to carry out the number of house parties you want to have. The hosts will want to see materials and know what help they will have from you.

The materials will have to be ready before the first phone call is made to the first potential host, and the first phone call needs to occur at least two months before the first party. So, the materials need to be produced in the next two weeks, hosts identified in a similar timeframe, calls made over a period of two or three months, and so on.

When you are tempted to skip planning, or to postpone planning until you "have some time," or to fly by the seat of your pants, just remember the Buddhist saying, "We have so little time, we must proceed very slowly."

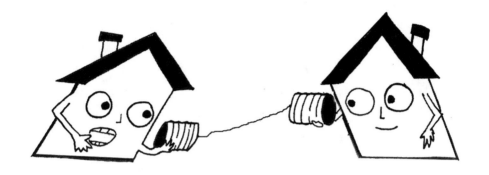

CHAPTER 8

MEDIA: CORPORATIONS CAN'T COMPETE WITH US

Paul Ryder

When it comes to communication media, corporations can't compete with community organizations:

- We own the most powerful communication medium that exists: word-of-mouth.

- We are already using the "new media" more effectively than polluters do, and we're just getting started.

- When our campaigns are in full swing, we can usually get good coverage in the mainstream media.

- In any medium, a company that has polluted the community's air for decades has a credibility problem that money cannot fix.

You wouldn't know this if you listened to the small army of columnists, commentators, think tank residents and academics who regularly announce the death of democracy. They note that in the last two decades, the number of corporations controlling most of the conventional U.S. news media dropped from fifty to only five: Time Warner, Disney, News Corporation, Bertelsmann, and Viacom.[1] They argue that this sharply narrows the range of viewpoints. These companies are also buying up each of the "new media" as soon as it is invented. Meanwhile, oil and chemical companies have big advertising and public relations budgets to spend on image-protection. And so on.

These are the arguments of media critics. There is some truth to them, of course, but we are not media critics. We are media practitioners. We use the media, and to do this, we have to look at the world differently. Rather than problems, we look for opportunities, and we find them as far as the eye can see.

---

1. Ben Bagdikian, *The New Media Monopoly* (Boston: Beacon Press, 2004).

1. Old media

Word-of-mouth

We start with a medium we take for granted. There are all kinds of media out there: newspaper, magazines, radio, telegrams, broadcast television, cable, Tivo, fax, ipod, cell phone, text messaging, VCR, DVD, email, web, and so on. Of these, the most powerful by far is the one we primarily use, word-of-mouth.[2]

There are many reasons why word-of-mouth is so powerful:

- The word "media" comes from the word meaning "middle". A medium—a radio or whatever—is in the middle between you and the person you are communicating with. It makes the communication possible, but it also limits it. With word-of-mouth, nothing is in the middle.

- Word-of-mouth is a two-way medium; the participants are equally able to contribute. By contrast, you can talk back to your radio if you want, but no one's going to hear you on the other end.

- Word-of-mouth cannot be controlled or censored.

- Word-of-mouth is self-propagating. The person receiving it can and will pass it on if they think it is worth passing on. It is highly democratic in that way.

Politicians know that if they become the target of late-night jokes by Jay Leno and David Letterman, their career is in deep trouble. Why? Not because of their direct influence: only 10 million people watch either show, in a nation of 298 million. Instead, it's because the monologues of these two performers are "water cooler material." They are suited for people to pass on to one another the next day on a work break. In other

---

2. Advertising agencies don't talk about word-of-mouth because they can't figure out how a company could buy it. If the company can't buy it, the ad agency can't collect its 15% commission.

words, they are influential because they can easily become word-of-mouth and then spread through the society.

The two people who best understand the power of word-of-mouth are Ben Affleck and Jennifer Lopez. It did not matter how much money the Sony Corporation spent on advertising their 2003 flop *Gigli*. It was flattened by word-of-mouth.

I didn't see that movie. Did you? Why not? Probably because someone told you they heard it was horrible.

Keep this in mind next time you start daydreaming, "What if we had a lot of money and we could buy time on television to get our message across and really be successful...?"

Stop and think again. Let's say your Uncle Chauncey dies and leaves you $10 billion. You have a meeting with your campaign planning group and say, "Now that we can afford to use any communications medium in the world, let's use the most powerful one out there. What is it? I remember. It is not television. It's the one we're already using: word-of-mouth."

The corporations we engage in our campaigns cannot compete with us in this medium, and in the places where we use it: front porches, living rooms, kitchens, and community meeting halls. That is our territory and that is where we win our campaigns.

Let's say a neighbor five houses down tells you she works in a plant and that the company that owns it is deliberately venting toxic chemicals in the middle of the night. Then you see a television ad saying that the company is "A Leader in Green Technology." Who are you going to believe?

In other words, we don't use word-of-mouth because we're poor, we use it because we're smart.

As an example of the power of word-of-mouth, consider how it can be used to prompt neighbors to use another ancient medium—handwritten letters—to help win campaigns.

Handwritten letters

During the Mittal Steel campaign in 2004, Ohio Citizen Action canvassers traveled all over the Cleveland area urging members to write steel plant manager William Brake about soot raining down on six surrounding neighborhoods. Within a few months, Brake had received thousands of handwritten letters, and a friend approached him at a high school football game to ask him why he was polluting Lake Erie.

Of course, most neighbor groups do not have the use of a full-time door-to-door canvass, but then again most campaigns don't involve a large metropolitan area.[3] In a smaller community, volunteer weekend canvassers can still have a successful letter-drive.

A walk-n-talk for letters

One way to encourage letter writing is through a walk-n-talk. These are fun, easy to organize, and productive.

The ingredients for a successful walk-n-talk are (1) a Saturday afternoon, (2) five volunteers (more is fine), (3) a flier with the latest news on the campaign and tips for neighbors on writing a good letter, (4) a map, with areas marked off for each volunteer or pair of volunteers to cover, and (5) pizza for afterwards.

The day starts with someone giving an upbeat welcome, campaign update, and description of how the day will go. Then a couple of volunteers teach everyone what should happen at a typical door by role-playing a few times.

Each volunteer gets a map, or if volunteers want to pair-up so they can do opposite sides of the streets, each pair gets a map. Then everyone heads out for three hours of walking and talking.

Where all the letters come from

If someone has ever promised you they would write a letter on an issue, you already know how small the chances are that the promised letter will get in the mail. It may be five percent, maybe less. It's not that they were lying to you, it's that ordinary obstacles of daily life got in the way.

---

3. With the help of a full-time door-to-door canvass during a two-year campaign, company executives have received as many as 10,000–25,000 handwritten letters from neighbors.

The secret of a successful walk-n-talk for letters is that you remove most of those obstacles. The following excerpt from a conversation at the door shows how:

"One of the most important things we're having people do today is write letters to the company president. Here is a flier with the latest news and some points on the back you can include on your letter if you want. It's really easy. What we need folks to do is to write these letters today and tape them to your door. I'm going to come back…"

"I don't know if I have time this afternoon. I've got a lot of errands…"

"That's OK, its really easy. That's why we have the points on the back. If you don't have a lot of time, you really just need to write a couple of sentences. 'Dear so-and-so: I'm a neighbor of the plant and I want you to clean up your act.' It could be something that simple. Just a simple sentence or two."

"OK. I'm not sure I have a stamp."

"No problem, don't need one. We'll provide the stamp and an envelope, too. Just the letter is what we need from you."

"OK."

"Thanks. We need to do it this afternoon because we're going to collect all the neighbors' letters together and mail them together. It makes a big impression that way too when they are all together like that."

"Or I could mail it. Could I just mail it myself on Monday?"

"Well, again, we want to make that bigger impression, and when we're able to get a few dozen letters together and put them on his desk all at the same time, he realizes, 'Uh-oh, I need to do something about this.' So it gets his attention. It really does work."

"When do you want it by?"

"3 o'clock, on the door."

"OK, I'll try to get it done."

"Thanks. I'm going to be walking around on foot, so I'm going to be making a special trip back, and really just a sentence or two if you don't have a lot of time. You don't have to type it, you can write it down on a sheet of paper. So can we definitely count on you to have something out there for us?"

"OK."

"And if you have kids and they want to sit down and do a drawing, too, we love that and that really makes a difference…"

"Drawing of what? What do you mean?"

"Drawing of the plant or of pollution or of their neighborhood, the way things should be, whatever they want to draw. It's really good."

"All right. Do I have to be here when you come back?"

"No, just tape it to the outside of the door. I won't even knock."

"OK."

"Great. Thanks."

The above is not just an ordinary conversation. It is the secret to a successful letter drive. It is worth studying and role-playing before the walk-n-talk crew goes out.

Note how many times the neighbor answering the door tries to slide out of a commitment, and how the canvasser brings them back every time in the most positive way. When the neighbor says the word "try," the canvasser reminds them that she is on foot and is making a special trip back, implying—again in the nicest way—that "try" is not a good enough answer.

If you learn this method, half to three-quarters of the people who promise you a letter will have it waiting for you when you come back. That is a lot better than five percent.

You are in for a treat when you see the letters people write. Even if, as above, they had been reluctant to make a commitment, once they set down to work, many people really open up and write what's on their minds. Not everyone, of course, but more than you might guess.

The pictures the kids draw are wonderful, all of them. What do you think will go through the mind of the company president when he or she sees them? Even little children in the community are appealing to them to clean up the mess they are making.

The communication may not end there, because many people still believe in the old-fashioned idea that handwritten letters deserve a reply. Company executives now have to make an executive decision: Do they ignore the letter, send a non-responsive form letter, or send an honest good-faith human reply?

Letter arithmetic

If 5 volunteers walk and talk for 3 hours, and each has 6 conversations an hour, that would be a total of 18 conversations per volunteer.[4] During those 18 conversations, the volunteer asks for a letter every time. Maybe 9 neighbors promise to write a letter, and 5 actually write it. So, if 5 volunteers bring back 5 letters each, that's 25 handwritten letters.

Your numbers may be different. Maybe your volunteers bring back 15 letters, not 25. That is not just OK; it is great. It is probably more handwritten letters than the company has received on any single issue ever. If there are children's pictures, that's another first. And that's just from one Saturday.

Are handwritten letters effective? When the company realizes they have a "public relations problem," they call in the experts, who follow a military approach. They see the neighbors as isolated passive targets for television, radio, newspapers and mail. They stand a safe distance away from the targets, firing messages in their direction. The more money the company has, the more messages it can bombard the community with.

The experts think the good-neighbor campaign is also separate from the community. Since the group does not have much money, they figure its media barrages will be feeble.

From the point of view of the neighborhood, things look different. The neighbors are not all that passive. Without waiting for anyone's permission, they have been talking to one another every day since the neighborhood was built. One of the things they have been talking about is the pollution coming from the plant, and the company's lies about it over the years. The company's statements do not carry much credibility with these

---

4. That is a rough estimate of contacts/hour for a Saturday afternoon. On a weekday evening, more people will be home to talk to, but it may be harder to find volunteers. You need to decide for yourself what time is best for your circumstances.

people. The local group is not a safe distance away; they are inside the neighborhood because they *are* the neighbors.

Before the company's public relations team can load its artillery, neighbors are already sending handwritten letters to the company. Such letters are much more powerful than a television ad or a form letter. By the time the company starts firing its messages into the neighborhood, it is too late. Their messages are landing on families who have lived with the problem, talked about it, and in some cases, already sent a letter to the company. At this point, advertising money is not the answer to the mess the company is in.

2. New media

New media arrive seemingly every week. As they show up, corporations try to figure out how to own them, governments try to figure out how to control them, and people get to work using them.

This is a worldwide trend with historic results:

- **1989:** Indigenous people in Brazil used portable video cameras to record meetings with government officials. "That way," says Ailton Krenak, director of the Union of Indigenous Nations, "we can catch their lies and make them hold true to their promises."[5] The tactics helped to "block a huge hydroelectric dam project that would have submerged tribal homelands."[6]

- **1989:** During the democracy protests in China, fax machines all over the country spewed out messages of support and uncensored news from overseas. "A sticker proclaiming 'Fax Saves Lives' was plastered over Hong Kong lampposts...In the wake of the Beijing massacre, Chinese authorities moved immediately to place all fax machines in the country under armed guard."[7]

---

5. Richard Zoglin, "Subversion by Cassette," *TIME* (September 11, 1989).
6. Adam Jones, "Communications Technology, Governance, and the Democratic Uprising," in Edward Connor, ed., *The Global Political Economy of Communication, Hegemony, Telecommunication and the Information Economy,* (London: Macmillan, 1994).

- **1991:** During a failed coup attempt in Moscow, the resistance organized itself—and prevailed—using the internet, even though only 3,000 computers in the former Soviet Union were then on-line.[8]

- **1998:** A nonviolent Indonesian student movement toppled the 32-year dictatorship of General Suharto. The president could not kill or imprison the movement's top leaders because there weren't any. It was a loose network held together by the internet.[9]

- **2006:** "China is cracking down on junk e-mail and 'illegal' mobile phone text messages, the official Xinhua News Agency said Tuesday....it appears part of China's efforts to discourage protests and restrict dissidents. Analysts say people in China and elsewhere have successfully used text messaging to organize, spread information and rally crowds of protesters."[10]

We're not trying to overthrow governments, but we can still use all these media and more to rein in the neighborhood polluter, no matter how big they are.

Email

For starters, if one of the group's members has a networked computer, they can use their email program to create a group list of everyone who wants to receive update emails about the campaign.[11] Then when it is time to alert people, the same email can go out to 10 or 50 people with one keystroke. Be sure that everyone on the list has asked to be on it; most people don't like unsolicited emails.

---

7. Ibid.
8. Ibid.
9. Bertil Lintner, Ashley Craddock, "Indonesia's Net War," *Wired News* (May 29, 1998).
10.*Associated Press*, (February 21, 2006).
11.With the Microsoft Outlook Express email program, go to tools > address book > file >new group. With the Mozilla Thunderbird email program, go to tools > address book > file > new > mailing list.

Even if many people in your group don't have email, it is still a time-saver to use it for those who do, and keep in touch with the others in other ways. Group emails are free, and you can keep adding new contacts for quite awhile before they become unwieldy.

Website

A website can be a powerful tool, but it is probably not the highest priority at the beginning of a campaign. The following are some considerations in deciding whether it is time to start one.

Think about the grassroots websites you have seen. There are two kinds.

The first kind is a brochure site. It gives the basic information on the organization or campaign, some background, and that is it. It may be beautifully designed or not, but its defining characteristic is that it never changes.

The other kind is a news site. It has all the information of a brochure site and it has all the campaign news on it, posted as soon as it happens. It changes all the time.

Most environmental websites are brochure sites. Unfortunately, a brochure site is worse than none at all. From the point of view of visitors to the site, it looks like nothing is going on in the campaign. That is a bad first impression. There will not be a second impression because nobody goes back to a brochure site a second time. Why bother? It is going to be the same as it was the first time.

Worst of all is a website that starts out with the best of intentions as a news site, but soon becomes a brochure site. We have all seen these. They have all the basic information, and a couple of news items. The date of the most recent item, however, is nine months ago. Here is proof positive to visitors that the campaign has died, even if it really hasn't.

So, in considering whether to have a website, the most important question is not money, technical expertise, or an appealing graphic design. It is whether someone is ready to commit the time to keep it current for the duration of the campaign. It could be your spouse, your teenage kid, or your sister. It could be an environmental club at the high school, or students at the local community college or university who want to do the web site as an independent project for credit.

Once you have solved this problem, the rest is not that hard.

Money. You can get free almost everything you need to run a website. Whoever volunteers to maintain the website either has a computer or knows how to get free access to one. Someone you know already has a copy of all the necessary software, or you can download it free from the internet. If you are thrifty, the only potential cost item is the server. This is a special computer permanently connected to the internet, and it serves up your web pages to people visiting your site. Maybe there is a local group with a website that will let you park your web pages on their server. Maybe a statewide environmental group will adopt your website. Maybe a friendly local internet firm will let you use space on their servers for free or at a big discount. As always, the secret is to ask.

Technical expertise. You do not need to find an expert to start a website. That is because the techniques are so simple, and the country is overrun with computer buffs who already know more than they need to set it up. They are all around you.

Design. You do not need to hire a web designer to come up with a sophisticated look for your site. No one expects your site to look like ESPN (Besides, you are doing something far more important than ESPN is doing). People want your site to be simple, clear and accurate. They want it to be the reliable authority on the issue. That is why everything you post must be solid. The site should be reserved for statements that you are ready to stand behind 100%.

And, of course, make sure that the most recent posting is prominent on the screen when your home page comes up, so visitors know immediately that it is a news site, not a brochure site.

The number of visitors to your site is not as important as who they are. Typically, they will be a mix of neighbors, reporters, company executives and employees, and government officials. You will know you're getting to the company when they try to introduce as an item for negotiation when you are going to "take that website down." Don't do it.

Scanning company documents

Exposing a company's inner workings to the public shocks the company as much as it does the public. These days it's an easy thing to do.

A sheet-fed document scanner with an automatic document feeder can take mountains of paper documents and turn them into searchable files for the web.[12] You can usually find such scanners at community colleges, universities, and law firms, or you can buy one at a reasonable price on eBay.

If, for example, the local polluter has been in a lawsuit that made public internal documents on their emissions, you may want to put them all on your website. The Environmental Working Group in Washington, D.C., used one of these machines to scan thousands of pages for their chemical industry archives project.[13]

To be safe, check with a friendly lawyer before posting internal company documents.

Digital still cameras

The easiest way to get still photos on your website is with a digital camera. You can load the images directly into a computer and then, with a little preparation, right onto your website. Digital cameras can now be found in 55% of American households.[14] Although this leaves out many households, you just need to find one person with a digital camera, and you're in business.

Even with a film camera, you can convert your film to digital images at drugstores or photo stores, or ask someone who has a scanner at home or work to convert a finished print into a computer file.

Then photograph everything related to the company, the pollution, the neighborhood, and the campaign, and post it on your site. People like to look at photos; it is hard to overdo it.

---

12. Commonly the documents are converted to "pdf" (portable document format) files. You can read pdf files with a program called Adobe Acrobat Reader, available for free download from http://www.adobe.com.
13. Environmental Working Group: http://www.ewg.org.
14. "Report," InfoTrends/CAP Ventures (July 14, 2005).

Digital video

The cost of digital video cameras, computers, and editing software has fallen drastically in recent years, such that this new media is also now within reach of community groups. It is up to you what to film: the condition of the plant, the latest fireball coming out of the stack, interviews with neighbors. You can copy the results to VHS tape or DVD disks and make dozens or hundreds of copies to send to neighbors, television stations, company executives, members of the company board of directors, and so on. In 2004, 92% of American households owned a VCR, and 76% owned a DVD player, so most people will be able to view it in one format or the other.[15] It does not matter if your camera-work is not ready for Hollywood; you are putting together evidence, not a feature film.

You will need technical help with this, so once you have an idea of what you want to do, take it to a video teacher at the high school or community college for advice on how to proceed.

If you have a short clip, 15–30 seconds, of an accident at the plant, for example, you can also put it on your website. Keep in mind that, as a practical matter, dial-up internet users will not be able to see the video. It just takes too long to download a big video file at the 56K dial-up speed. More people are shifting to high-speed broadband connections every month: "In January 2005, 103.8 million Americans had broadband access; by August, that figure had grown to 120.8 million."[16] Still, it is good manners to note the file size next to the video link to warn people using dial-up connections.

You might be careful where you stand when taking pictures. News photographers know that as long as they are on public land, such as the sidewalk, and they are not using powerful telephoto lenses to "see" inside buildings that are ordinarily hidden from public view, they are not invading privacy or trespassing.

---

15. Pew Research Center for People and the Press, press release (June 8, 2004).
16. Nielsen/NetRatings, Inc., *NetSpeed Report* (September 28, 2005). "Broadband users" are those with a Digital Subscriber Line (DSL), cable modem, wireless connection, or fiber (T-1) connection.

3. Using conventional media: television, radio and newspapers

The old and new media described above can be enough to win a campaign without any help from conventional media: television, radio and newspapers.

If we think of conventional media as a bonus, we won't be disappointed if our campaign is not covered by it. If it does cover the campaign, it is a nice surprise.

If we do things right, we will probably be covered. We can't force it, though: When a campaign is struggling, it is tempting to think: "What does a successful campaign look like? I know. A successful campaign gets in the media. So maybe if we can get some media, it'll help the campaign."

This line of thinking leads to two errors.

The first error is to buy television, radio or newspaper ads. Since these are costly, someone has to stop working on the campaign to fundraise to pay for it. If they raise the money, the ad it buys will take its place among the other ads the average person is subjected to each day: 108 television ads, 34 radio ads and 112 print ads.[17] Then it is over. Except for a few people's fading memory of the ad, the campaign is in the same sad state it was in when you left it.[18]

The second error is to stage a "media event," also known as a "press hit," which is really a non-event with a concocted visual—a prop, backdrop, maybe a costume and antics—to trick the television stations into covering it. This tactic is based on the idea that if television stations want to cover water-skiing squirrels, then that's what we'll give them.

---

17. Estimate from Advertising Media Internet Center, 470 Park Avenue South, 15th floor, New York, New York 10016, www.amic.com.

18. This is not to say such ads are always a mistake. If they directly advance the campaign, they can be useful. For example, if the campaign has just enlisted the support of an important new constituency, such as local religious leaders, the best way to announce it might be an open letter from them to the company president printed as an ad in the daily newspaper. Television, radio, or newspaper ads are a mistake when they are undertaken just to "get some media."

If the visual is startling, the hit might get on television, but over time this tactic defeats itself. Your organization gets a reputation as a group that fakes it. It becomes harder to get coverage for each successive hit, and rightly so. When you finally do have some real news, no one will believe you.

Instead of trying to force media coverage, let it come to you. If your campaign is going well, the real action driving the campaign will include genuinely newsworthy elements, and the media will want to cover it. Then the conventional media becomes our media, too.

If your campaign isn't newsworthy right now, the best use of your time is to concentrate on getting the campaign in gear.

When the time comes to help the press cover your campaign, you will need to know their rules and follow them. That is what the next chapter is about.

CHAPTER 9

▼

PUBLICITY TIPS

Paul Ryder

"But isn't this a David and Goliath thing?"

A reporter actually asked me this once, meaning that he thought my group's situation was hopeless and we should give up. I said, "Yes. That's why we expect to win."

By repeating the question here, I am not primarily urging that reporters get better acquainted with the Bible, although it wouldn't hurt: David beat Goliath in a first-round knockout. Instead, I want to emphasize that neighbors who talk to reporters need to be prepared to respond to all kinds of questions.

Preparation is 90% of presswork, and this chapter helps you prepare by understanding better how the press works.

1. Working with the press

Reporters

You will get much better press if you have good working relationships with reporters. It is essential to get to know them, what they're interested in, what they're reporting about. Who's new? Who left town? Who likes whom? Whom do you need to cultivate? Who will lead you to someone you want to get to know?

However you keep track of activists and potential activists, do the same with the reporters. Every library has media guides, but they are often out of date because reporters usually come and go quickly.

Reporters work hard and on deadline. Their phones are constantly ringing. It's important to respect their time.

- When they call, call back quickly.

- If you're not sure of the answer, ask them what their deadline is and let them know when you will call back with the answer. Never say something you are unsure of; it may be embarrassing to read it the next day when you know it is wrong.

- If a radio reporter calls, they may want to tape you while you are talking. If you're not fully prepared, tell them you'll call back in 10 minutes. That will give you time to clear everyone out of the room, put your notes and facts in front of you and get ready.

- When you call a reporter, begin with "Hello, this is.... I wanted to tell you about.... Do you have a minute? No? When would be a good time for you?"

- Some reporters are new and starting from scratch. They have little job security, and so may be less willing to pursue controversial stories. They sometimes appreciate a background briefing on an issue they are going to have to cover.

- Do not attack the media; it will backfire on you. If there is a big problem with a story, talk to the reporter one-on-one. Let's say you ignore this advice and complain about a reporter to their editor. The reporter will find out about it when their editor says, "What's this all about?" The reporter will proceed to rip you. Having started with one bad story, you now have one bad story, one bitter reporter who cannot wait to write a second bad story, and one editor who has just heard an earful of bad things about you.

How to become a source

Reporters are looking for facts or sources who can give them more facts, perspective and opinion. When you are brand new, you may not be seen as a source because you do not fit the profile. You do not speak for a business, a politician, a government agency, or any other part of the establishment. So, at the beginning, give them facts, and enlist people they already regard as sources.

You always want to give them solid facts, but your goal over time is to become a source for the reporter as well. This happens when you develop a record of having your facts straight, showing good judgment, being quotable, and helping them with story ideas, leads on developing stories, and other contacts. And, above all, it will happen when you and the reporter develop a good working relationship.

Most reporters want to find a second source (government official, academic, etc.) to confirm any controversial information you present. Part of preparation is thinking of such sources to suggest. Also, give the reporter the names and phone numbers of people who will disagree with you. You will be helping the reporter find conflict, thus making the story more newsworthy, and it will earn you credibility points with the reporter.

If a celebrity or an important person is in town, help them get to meet them. Over time, they start to call you to ask for these things, and you become a trusted source.

As a source, you are more likely to be covered when you react quickly to today's news, calling the reporter with a comment. Important stories roll out over several days as further developments occur. Reporters refer to the articles as the "day-one story," "day-two story," and so on. Be sure to call in time to be in the day-one story, because your opinions alone likely will not merit a day-two story. You might get a day-two story by taking some action, for example, a legal filing, a delegation call for a meeting with an official, or a formal demand for an investigation. These sometimes take less research and preparation than you might think.

You won't become a trusted source if a reporter finds that you are vague on the facts, or slant them, claim that you speak for more people than you do, distort what your opponent said, make threats you have no intention or ability to carry out, or peddle weak stories.

Again, a candid "I don't know" once in a while does wonders for your credibility with the reporter.

What is newsworthy?

Reporters and editors define what's newsworthy, not you. Don't waste time whining about this fact of life. Learn to thrive under it. It is easy to learn what local reporters and editors think is newsworthy: just read them every day.

Think from a reporter's point of view. Is it newsworthy? What would be the headline if you were writing an article about this? What would be the first sentence of it? What do you expect listeners to remember about this?

Is it new and different? Is it something that no one has done before? Is it something that is happening now or tomorrow? Does it involve action or conflict, a clash of people or ideas?

Are prominent people involved? Is it odd or unbelievable? Are there significant consequences, especially local consequences? Look for the human angle. Find out how your campaign affects people. After all, a good reporter tries to tell the people who read the newspaper and watch television news why they should care enough to read or listen to the story.

Daily newspapers

Print is the major source of news for news and assignment editors for television and radio. They come in to work in the morning and open up the newspaper to see what is news; then they decide what news to cover.

Reading the paper every day will also tell you who is covering your issues. They frequently reshuffle assignments. Do not forget local columnists, who frequently have wide scope for topics. (A columnist typically has a mug shot that runs beside his stories, which includes analysis or opinion. News reporters are supposed to be unbiased, and they are largely anonymous.)

The same campaign can have different angles of interest to different reporters. For example, aspects of a pesticide campaign can be of interest to reporters covering business, farming, outdoors, food, politics, or suburbia. In addition, the editorial staff might be interested in running an opinion piece.

Some print reporters will appreciate it if you send them a related article they might have missed, with a "thought you might be interested" note. By sending it to them by mail, rather than calling them with it, you will be showing that you respect their time. Many reporters are touchy about getting too much email, too. They get a lot these days. It is best to ask each one how they want to hear from you.

Op-eds

An op-ed is so named because it is an opinion piece that appears *opposite* the *editorial* page of a newspaper. it is sometimes called a "guest column."

One occasion for writing an op-ed is at the beginning of the campaign. Just call the editorial page editor to suggest it. If she agrees, ask how many words it should be and write to length.

Another occasion for writing an op-ed is after an attack on your group in an editorial or an op-ed. Call the paper the same day an attack appears to ask for a chance to respond.

In reply, resist at all costs the three great temptations:

Temptation #1: Repeating the negative comments about you or the organization that appeared in the original piece.

Temptation #2: Being defensive.

Temptation #3: Attacking the newspaper or the author of the attack.

Instead, once the paper has agreed to give you space, think about how you would most like to fill it. Why waste it on snappy comebacks when you can deliver the best positive message on the issue? Most of the people who read your op-ed won't even remember the original piece, let alone its specific points.

Preface your reply with something neutral such as, "Concerning your June 21 editorial on incinerators…" Then tell people why you are passionate about your campaign, and why they should be too. Do not forget to include somewhere the name of your organization or campaign.

The three temptations are so strong that it is essential that you ask someone else to review your draft.

Weekly newspapers

Community and neighborhood newspapers are widely read. The *Sun* newspaper chain in the Cleveland area, for example, has a combined circulation of 200,000. On local issues, some weeklies have more credibility with readers than the major daily newspapers.

Weeklies are local, so all stories you offer them must have a local angle. Read them regularly to get a feel for what they want, and tailor stories specifically to them. Mentioning area residents by name can make the difference in getting the story printed. 90% of releases are not localized, according to a 1993 study. Newspapers published 78 of 174 localized releases, and only 87 of 1,774 non-localized releases, according to another study. Thus, newspapers were nine times more likely to publish localized releases than non-localized ones.

Weeklies need more lead-time than a daily. Find out their deadline and give them plenty of slack.

Weeklies are short on photographers and are sometimes willing to print photographs provided by others. Ask them. Again, localizing is every-thing—make sure local residents are in the photo and the caption.

Make sure the photos are great. Action shots are best. Many people know what they are doing with a camera. The best thing is to find one or more who are willing to help by taking pictures for you, rather than you trying to learn it yourself. There is a lot to it, and while newspapers will use amateurish photos, you will do your cause more good with a terrific shot that catches people's attention.

Radio

Radio is a powerful medium, and all radio news wants is a voice. Once every two or three months, listen to all the radio stations on the dial so you stay current on their format and audience. You'll find very few with real reporters any more. If a station has news at all, it is usually a combination of "rip and read" from the morning newspaper, and radio actualities. An "actuality" is the sound of news being made that the station has on tape and inserts into the news report. It might be a clip of a phone interview with a newsmaker—maybe you. Or, somebody may have taped the sounds of the local turkey farm and the radio is playing it as part of a story on sur-prise health inspections.

Don't call a radio newscaster during drive time. No calls before 9:00 A.M., or between 4:00 PM and 6:00 P.M. Mornings are busy and there are fewer reporters working. Five minutes after a newscast is the best time to call.

Get help

There are many great publicity projects: maintaining a speaker's bureau or experts bank, producing a local newsletter, researching and writing fea-ture stories, or working with editorial boards, op-eds, letters to the editor, columns in special publications, photos and video, and so on. It is a great way for a volunteer, or several, to make a difference.

2. Press releases

Not all news requires a press release. Sometimes, you may want to single out one or two reporters and approach them individually with a news idea. If they are interested, give them the necessary raw materials, and they can get to work without a press release. A release does have the advantage, however, of reducing potential confusion by putting everything in writing, and you know that every reporter got the same information from you at the same time.

If you want to do a press release, here's how:

Format

- Paper: Use 8 1/2" x 11" letterhead, with 1" left and right margins, one-sided, double-spaced. This is to let reporters edit right on your release before they type it up. If they can't fit their editing on your release, they will have to start from scratch on their keyboard, and the article will be less like your release.

- Release date: In the upper right hand corner, type "FOR IMMEDI-ATE RELEASE: [TODAY'S DATE]".

- Contacts: Just below the release date, in the right hand side, type "CONTACT: [NAME AND PHONE NUMBER OF SPOKES-PERSON OR SPOKESPEOPLE]." If possible, include the home, office, and cell phone number of each spokesperson as well as their email addresses.

- Headline: Skip a few lines and type the headline, centered on a single line. Use a strong verb. "Hundreds march on City Hall" is a better headline than "Rally at City Hall."

- Dateline: The dateline is the city in which your press release originates. Name it, in all capital letters, on the same line the first sentence begins.

- Start with what's newsworthy. "Burying the lead" is the error of putting the news anywhere else but in the first sentence. If you have two or more different things you think are the news, force yourself to make a single choice. It should be simple, straightforward, and in plain English. Even if you put something in the headline, you also need to put it into the first sentence. Editors almost never use your headline, and you don't want the story stripped of a key point.

- Make up a catchy quote or two and attribute them to the group's main spokesperson. Work into the attribution a description of the organization. A good reporter will call that spokesperson for an interview anyway, and a lazy one will just run with the quote you have provided. For example, "This campaign will clean up the playground where dozens of small children play daily," said Sandy Buchanan, executive director of Ohio Citizen Action, the state's largest environmental organization, with 100,000 members."

- Body: Add essential details and background, but the whole release should not be longer than two pages. If you have additional material such as a list or chart, put it in an attachment. Order the items by diminishing importance, so editors can cut the story from the bottom. It does not have to read like an essay. Include a paragraph on what you want the reader, listener, or viewer to do as a result of reading or hearing about your story: "Call for more information: 555-5555." "Tickets can be bought at the door."

- Last paragraph: A boilerplate sentence or two describing the organization or project. If you mention another organization you are working with, include organizational boilerplate from them, too.

- End: At the end of the release, center the following: ###

Style

- Write the release in journalistic style, as though you were the reporter. It is not a statement by you, it is a pretend news article and it should appear to be factual, not opinionated. All opinions should come with quotation marks or paraphrase, and attribution to a source.

- Write as though the reader knows nothing about the issue, and none of the background.

- Please, no acronyms. A certain proportion of the readers will not know what you are talking about.

- Indent paragraphs, and justify text on the left only. Keep paragraphs short, and do not split a paragraph between pages one and two.

- If it is a two-page release, center the following at the bottom of page one: "(MORE)". Add a header to the top of p.2, with the headline, date and page number.

- When in doubt, follow the journalists' rules, for grammar, spelling, punctuation and style, the *Associated Press Stylebook*.[1]

- Who is going to receive this release? Have you done tailored versions of the release for different media outlets?

- Are you prepared to stand behind every fact in the release? If you are not certain that a fact is true, that you know the source, and that the source is solid, take it out.

- Ask someone else to proof it after you think it looks perfect. Don't put out a release with the slightest mistake of content or form in it.

Delivering the release

Morning dailies. Between 8:00 A.M. and 2:00 PM is a good time to deliver releases. The deadline for the next day's paper can be as early as 4:00 PM the previous afternoon, so, if you deliver a release after 2:00 PM, you will be pushing the reporter against the deadline.

Radio. A 2:00–3:00 PM story for the next day works best.

---

1. Goldstein, Norm, ed., *Associated Press Stylebook and Briefing on Media Law* (New York: Perseus Books, 2005).

Television. television assignment meetings happen early in the day, so if you want your release to be considered for the six o'clock news, you'll need to drop it off very early in the day. If your release is for the next day, you can deliver the release to the television station in mid-afternoon. For television and radio, address the release to the assignment editor. They are like the city editor on a newspaper. They look over the day's releases, wire service copy, and other sources, and assign a crew. News directors are far removed from the news; they are administrators worrying about budgets. The priority should be assignment editors, managing editors at television stations that have them, and then news directors.

When you are sending releases or advisories for weekend action, address them to the "weekend assignment editor." You can't rely on the regular assignment editor passing them on. It is probably best to call first and find out who these people are, and address the release with the correct spelling of their name.

You can send a release to two people at one outlet, but handwrite a note on it that says, "I've also sent this to…" so they can coordinate. Sometimes send a release to someone you know won't write it up, just to keep them informed.

Faxing is easy and gives immediacy, so it is tempting to fax the release and leave it at that. If possible, however, stop at the newspapers to hand deliver the release, so you can talk to the reporter and get to know them face to face, learn who and what they cover. If you fax, call first. Then, call the reporter to follow-up the release.

3. Helping the press cover our campaign

When your campaign is about to take an action that the press might find newsworthy, here is how to help them cover it.

Four days before the action

- Choose a time. If you have control over the timing of the action, choose from 11:00 AM–2:00 PM on a day early in the week. By the end of the week, many reporters and editors are busy putting together Sunday and weekend editions. Mondays are good days for news conferences because they are generally slower news days. With the demise of afternoon newspapers and with the increased importance of local television news, early afternoons make the most sense. On a typical day there will be several news events scheduled at 10:00 AM, so it is better to go a little later. The evening has its charms, too. Local television news shows are proliferating beyond all reason and they may be looking for material in the evenings. In addition, for the few remaining radio stations that concentrate on news, the morning drive time is prime time, and is staffed into the evening.

- Choose and visit a place. If you can, plan the action within 10 or 15 minutes of downtown, so reporters and news crews can get there easily. You must personally visit the place and check it out thoroughly: electric outlets, a podium, photo angles, everything.

- Choose all speakers, a host for the event, and another staff to assist the host. Limit speakers to no more than three; one or two are much better. All speakers should agree at the outset that they will immediately follow-up the event with phone calls. Choose a spokesperson who can appear comfortable in front of a camera, project credibility, know the issues, have the self-discipline to stop talking, and be willing to prepare thoroughly. Make sure they are prepared for questions and answers. Prepare "sound bites," brief quotes of no more than 15 seconds that will play well on television and radio. The speaker should practice saying these so that they flow well when the tape is rolling.

- First draft of press release

- Choose graphics and decide how you're going to produce them. Don't forget organizational visuals, such as a banner or logo.

- Find a photographer, not you, to shoot the action. A digital camera is desirable, so they can email the best shots to the community paper with a complete caption, immediately.

Two days before

- News advisory: If appropriate, drop and fax a media advisory to all media you want to cover the action. To television news stations, address to "news planning desk." Include in the media advisory all the necessary information. Title it "ADVISORY," centered, followed by the four "W's": who, what, when, and where. Give enough description of the event to persuade them to want to come, but not enough to enable them to cover it without showing up. For television, this means describing the visual and the location, and providing a contact name and number.

One day before

- Make relentless follow-up calls. Did they get the advisory? If not, fax another. Give a prepared 20 second pitch on why they will be happy they showed up.

- Final changes to press release

- Based on expected turnout plus extras, duplicate press release, copies of other materials.

- Finish graphics, materials preparation. Include in the materials a media kit, including background on the issue, a bio of the speaker, a black and white photo of the speaker (for weekly newspapers only), a copy of the release, and a description of the organization.

- Spend time checking out the site. What is the set up? What will the cameras see? Where will the speaker stand? What will be behind the speaker? How will you handle the graphics? Do you need to mount them? Do you need electric outlets and where are they? If necessary, when can you get to the site the day of the action? When will you have to leave the site? Who is the contact at the site the day of the event? What is the nearest phone number at the site?

- Ask a volunteer with a VCR to tape your story on the local news so you will have a copy to show others who missed it.

- Review everything with all participants.

Day of event

- Re-call media.

- Arrive at the site 45 minutes too early. Assume everything will go wrong.

- The host meets and identifies reporters, has a list of invitees and checks off their names, adds others you did not expect, distributes press releases and other materials, and makes sure that the media has what they need, such as help finding the electric outlets. The host also keeps the speaker apprised of who has arrived, and helps the spokesperson decide when to begin.

- There should be another person available to help, getting misplaced materials at the last minute, delivering messages, etc.

- After the action, make a list of television, radio, and print reporters who couldn't make it, and divide up calls between speakers. Radio will be happy to have a chance to do an actuality. Maybe television will invite you over for a live interview on the local evening news, or a one-on-one taping, known as a "stand up." Maybe print reporters will admit they have lost your release, and you can fax them another.

- These follow-up calls are crucial, and may take a couple of hours to finish, so please be sure all speakers have committed in advance to spending the time. Be with them when they sit down to make the calls and don't let them leave until they're done.

- Call people who have agreed to videotape the news and tell them what television stations covered it.

Follow-up

- Thank everybody who participated.

- Make sure you collect all print and video news clips and give or show them to anyone who could conceivably want to see them.

- The follow-up to the event is important to developing your relationships with the reporters, starting with it being a good reason to be back in touch with them. Did they get all the information they needed?

- Commend reporters if their story is accurate. Remember, they do not want to hear you praise them for siding with you in the conflict. That would be unprofessional of them. Their job is not to take sides, but to write thorough accurate stories.

- If you've received feedback from the community about the story, let them know.

- If you feel you have been misquoted, grow a thick skin, but let them know in a nice way if there are major errors in the story.

- Keep good notes about which reporters and media outlets responded. This will come in handy for you and others.

4. Interviews

The big secret of successful speakers is preparation and practice. Anyone can do it.

Prepare

What is your agenda for the interview? You may only get 15 seconds on the air, so decide what is the one point you want to deliver. Make sure it includes a fact or an example so people will have something to remember.

What is the reporter's agenda? What will the reporter think are the weak points in your message? The question you dread is the question they will ask, so decide what question that is, choose your answer, and practice it.

In an interview, the reporter and editor seem to be all-powerful since they get to ask the questions and cut the tape. It's not so. You can get your point on the air if you can discipline yourself. Almost no one can speak naturally in colorful 15-second sound bites, so write them out and learn them. Once you have a draft, give it the same scrutiny you would give a lead in a press release. Give answers that are responsive and tie everything back to your main point. Throw in another fact or example, and get back to the point. There is no shame in being repetitive. Make sure every answer stops at 20 seconds, because anything longer will be cut. If you do this, you will be giving the tape editor little choice of what to pick, since all your answers lead back to your point.

Part of preparation is deciding how you want to come across. Sometimes grassroots spokespeople try to come across like policy experts. Corporate and government officials invented policy-talk to cover up their activities. If you talk that way, viewers will assume you are somehow in on the cover-up. Don't try to be a junior scientist. Instead, be what you already are, a human being who knows what you are talking about.

Practice

Practice by yourself and then with another person and a video camera. Ask around: Someone you know has one and cannot wait to use it. The camera is such a powerful tool that you and your friend won't need an expert to tell you what's wrong.

You'll be able to diagnose your own technique problems: leaning on the lectern, swaying, swiveling, shifting from one foot to the other, poor posture, touching your face, gesturing too much or too little, talking too fast, fidgeting with your papers, putting your hands in your pockets, folding your arms, making quotation mark gestures with your index fingers, speaking monotonously, saying "um," "ah," or "uh," and so on. All this will be obvious.

- Speak more slowly than usual and smile.

- Look into your interviewer's eyes. Let the camera find you, not vice versa.

- If there's a danger that you will give a defensive response, stop and be silent briefly. It will be just long enough for you to come up with a positive answer. This also helps if you have a problem with "ums" and "ahs." Take three or four seconds to think about the question before you answer. This is tape, and the silence will be edited out.

- Don't lie or even exaggerate. If the unadorned facts aren't compelling, why are you working on this issue?

- Don't ask to go off the record, and if a reporter suggests it, turn them down. Some people think it's savvy to tie themselves in knots over distinctions between "off-the-record," "on background," "not for attribution," and "deep background." Forget these fictional categories. There is only one mode: on the record. The reporter will respect you for it, and you and your organization will not be burned.

- If the question includes negative comments about the organization or your positions on the issues, don't repeat them in your answer. The question probably was not going on the air anyway. The way it can get on the air is in your answer: "No, I'm not the town crackpot, in fact…" And many viewers will remember: "…town crackpot…."

Once you have practiced the technique, think about the tape you just made from the perspective of the editor back at the station.

The editor will cut out all the questions posed to you and any answer longer than at most 20 seconds. Will your main point be left? Have you given the editor a piece of tape in which you repeat negative points in the question, or in which you are led away from your message, failing to tie your answers back to your main point? What, if anything, will the editor end up putting on the air?

CHAPTER 10

▼

TALKING WITH THE
COMPANY

Paul Ryder

1. "Why should we talk to them at all?"

The idea of talking to the company often prompts the following reaction from the neighbors: "Why should we talk to them at all? Why give them credibility? You can't cut deals with liars. They ought to be on trial. Negotiations lead to compromise and we're not going to compromise our principles. How can you think of trusting them?"

Some neighbors may declare their commitment to the cause this way: "I'll do anything. I'll go to jail, I don't care." "Anything?" "Yes." "Would you talk with the company president?"

"No way. After the way he has treated us, are you kidding? No."

Meanwhile, at the company headquarters, executives are saying, "Why should we talk to them at all? I'm trying to keep my people employed. I don't have time to get yelled at by a bunch of chronic complainers."

The pollution has created a poisonous atmosphere in more ways than one.

Deciding whether to talk to the company requires remembering that your goals are to make the neighborhood healthier and safer, and to make sure this never happens again by creating a working relationship between neighbors and the company.

If talking to the company could help achieve these goals, isn't it worth it?

But, after everything that's happened, how can we trust the company to honor any agreement they make? That's a good question. In fact, trust is not required for a successful outcome, or even a long-term constructive relationship with the company. People in every walk of life all over the world have working relationships with people they do not necessarily trust all that much. Trust makes everything much easier of course, but it is not necessary.

To make it work, people rely on the Russian saying, "Trust but verify," and that is just how good neighbor campaigns succeed, as you'll see later in this chapter.

In many conflicts, talking takes place only in a concentrated and carefully choreographed process called "negotiation." Sometimes negotiations come at a prescribed time, as at the end of a contract, and sometimes they come at the end of a long period of pointless fighting.

Good neighbor campaigns don't restrict themselves this way. At the beginning of a campaign, neighbors open up lines of communication with everyone they can at the company, from the CEO or plant manager to their secretaries to board members to engineers to union officials and rank and file employees. They keep these lines open throughout the campaign.

This communication is a way to learn about how the company operates, its history, how it makes decisions and how it is reacting to the campaign. At the same time, it is a way to help the company executives understand the neighbors' perspective better, see that they have many interests in common, and realize that the good neighbor campaign will not stop growing until the company acts in good faith to solve the problem.

2. Getting to Yes

Our approach to talking with the company is adapted from a book, *Getting to Yes,* by the Harvard Negotiation Project.[1] It is short, easy to read and full of good examples. The book is a business best seller, so many executives will have already read it and you won't have to teach it to them from scratch. The following summary is no substitute for reading the book.

The authors first explain why the usual way people negotiate doesn't work very well, and then describe a better way.

The conventional method can be called "positional negotiating," because each side seizes a position, defends it, and assaults the other's position. "Not one penny more!" "Not one penny less!"

Neither side has a thought-out reason for picking their position. It is just somehow what they feel they want, or the most they think they can get by arguing. After some back and forth, maybe one or both sides storm out and there's no deal, or maybe they split the difference between their mindless positions.

Was it a good deal? Who knows? Both sides were pulling numbers out of their ears.

---

1. Roger Fisher, William Ury, Bruce Patton, Harvard Negotiation Project, *Getting to Yes* (New York: Penguin, 1991). It is available in the business section of libraries and bookstores. At the end of 2005, Amazon.com was selling used soft cover copies of this book for $2.24.

Did it develop a working relationship such that they could do business again in the future? Maybe not, because if they compromised, it proved that each of their original "won't budge" positions was a lie.

Some positional bargainers think they are savvy because they show up with a "bottom line," the position past which they really won't compromise further. This still does not answer where any of these positions came from.

Luckily, there is an alternative to this mess. "Interest negotiation" is based on the idea that a successful negotiation produces two outcomes. First, the agreement advances the interests of both parties as much as possible. Second, it leaves the relationship between the parties in good working order. In other words, they will be able to conduct productive negotiations when something comes up in the future.

This approach starts by "separating people from the problem." Typically, both parties bring a lot of baggage to the negotiating table. They have trouble discussing the merits because they can't stop thinking about misunderstandings, attitudes, past insults, people they know who have been mistreated, lies, and so on.

Get this on the table first. Sometimes just saying it is enough. Sometimes misunderstandings can be straightened out. Mistakes can be acknowledged and corrected. Insults can be taken back. However it goes, this must come first, before you address the merits. Otherwise, it will keep bubbling up in disruptive ways.

This done, the discussion can turn to examining each party's interests. Interests are not the same as positions. One of the neighbors' interests might be, for example, that their children not breathe chemicals that trigger asthma attacks. A position—also known as a 'demand'—might be that the company buy and install a certain piece of pollution control equipment.

The neighbors may think this position is the only way to meet their interests. They may be wrong; there may be many other ways to do this. For example, maybe the company could change their manufacturing process so that the asthma-trigger chemical is not used at all. This may be cheaper for the company than buying the pollution control equipment, and may even be more profitable than the current process.

Let's consider a different position. The neighbors could insist that emissions of this chemical be cut by 75% over five years. It sounds like a strong demand, but is it? If the company can change its process to eliminate that chemical, that would be a 100% cut in emissions in less than five years.

The advantage of discussing interests rather than positions, then, is that you bring the company into the discussion, and invite them to suggest options for meeting those interests in a way that you had no idea was possible. The more options on the table, the more likely it is that both parties can agree on one of them.

Some people find it easier to think up positions than to define their interests. The way to discover your interests is to take a position, and start asking why.

"We demand that the company install the X-100 filter."

"Why?"

"So the plant will emit less of this chemical."

"Why is that important to you?"

"Because my daughter keeps having asthma attacks."

Now we know what the interest is.

The neighbors have a number of interests and so does the company. You can put them into three categories: (1) interests that the neighbors and the company have in common, (2) interests that may differ but do not conflict, and (3) interests that do conflict.

The more interests you can put in the first two categories, the better. The best outcome is to have everything in the first two categories, but this may not always be possible.

For anything in the third category, it helps to find objective standards both parties can agree on, such as precedents elsewhere, court decisions, views of respected authorities, market tests, the technological state of the art, and so on.

This method produces much better decisions, and can create a long-term working relationship. It also frees you from the apparatus of positional negotiating: no demands, no positions, no bottom line, no tricks, no threats, no surprises, no lying, no contests of will, no sides, and no concessions. It's more like problem-solving.

3. Preparation

There are many things for you to sort out before meeting with the company. Among the most important is your relationship with the company.

This relationship is not at all like that of two strangers haggling over the price of an old lamp. The neighbors and the company are not strangers. Even if they don't know one another's names, they already have a relationship and it is terrible. Every interaction between neighbors and the company illustrates what's wrong.

Consider a letter from fenceline neighbors to the plant manager, starting like this, "We request a meeting to discuss our concerns."

Here's the first problem: A subordinate uses the word "request" in speaking to a superior. Between equals, it would be, "We invite you to meet with us," "I propose we meet," "I think we should meet," or more familiarly, "Let's meet."

If you are relaxing in your backyard and an old toaster-oven comes flying over the fence and lands next to you, would you go to see your next-door neighbor and say, "I request a meeting"? I don't think you would. You might say, "Excuse me, I need to talk to you." You might say something else, but I am sure the word "request" would not be in the sentence.

Using the word "request" is a declaration of inferiority in the very first sentence.

There is an old-fashioned word "supplicant," from the word "ply," meaning "to fold" or "to bend." What is bended is your knee. To be a supplicant is to go to someone on bended knee.

Remember that scene from *The Godfather* movie? Don Corleone sits in a darkened room and people approach, hat in hand, requesting an audience, kissing his ring, asking for favors. They are supplicants. These are dominance and submission rituals. It is like a television nature show, where the alpha male ape stretches out his spine to look down on a cringing subordinate.

Company executives don't mind being treated this way. After all, alpha males make the decisions that supplicants have to put up with.

There is a second way neighbors sometimes approach the company: in a state of fury. It is understandable given what's happened, but it is not effective. Companies know how to deal with angry neighbors without much difficulty.

If the neighbors are too furious to talk to company executives, that's OK because the executives didn't want to talk to them anyway. If a neighbor loses his temper in a community meeting, that's OK, too. It will isolate him as unreasonable.

Therefore, the company has no trouble dealing with both submissive and belligerent neighbors.

There is a third way. Good neighbor campaigns undermine this sick psychology by approaching company managers as equals. They are neighbors just like us. We don't throw tons of soot over the back fence into their yard, and we expect the same courtesy from them.

We show company officials all the respect any human being deserves, regardless of what they have done, but we do not go to them or anyone else on bended knee.

Let's go back and take another look at that same first sentence from the letter. "We request a meeting to discuss our concerns…" The phrase "our concerns" takes us into the arena of sexual politics.

To see why, take a hypothetical domestic problem: He won't pick up after himself. She reminds him patiently over and over, to no effect. After weeks of this, she says, "We need to talk." Being perceptive, she realizes that there are now three problems, not one. First, the house is a mess. Second, their relationship is a mess, since he has been ignoring her for weeks. Third, she is furious.

He does not want to discuss any of the three problems. He thinks, "Maybe if I can do something about her emotions, I can get a pass on the other two problems. Maybe I'll get her some candy and flowers, or take her out for dinner."

A good-neighbor campaign has some of the same dynamics. Most plant managers would rather not meet with neighbors at all. By the time of the first meeting, there are the same three problems: pollution, a bad relationship, and anger.

And, too often, the company executive does his level best to change the problem they are discussing from pollution to emotions.

"We want you to *feel good* about living near the plant."

"We want you to *be comfortable* about what we're doing."

"We want to alleviate your *anxiety*."

"We want to understand *your concerns*."

In other words, we in management live in the real world. You neighbors live in a world of emotions. We are willing to come down to your level and help you stabilize your emotions, so we can get back to business. Not only do company executives talk like this; you may notice that government officials do as well.

The way to counter this is to guide the executive back to the topic, politely, firmly, and repeatedly. And the topic is not our emotions, but the reality that his chemicals have found their way into our children's lungs.

If this company tactic is worth deflecting, it is also a good idea not to bring it up in the first place. Why start your first communication with the company by identifying the issue as a *"concern"*? It is better to get right to the point. "We are writing to invite you to meet with us to discuss the soot crossing your fenceline into the neighborhood."

As these two examples show—from the first sentence in your first letter—the place to start changing your relationship with the company is in your own mind.

4. Stages

At first, the company does not take the neighbors seriously. Often the executives refuse to speak with them at all. If they do communicate, it may be through a public relations staff, a community affairs liaison, or an environmental official. Although the environmental official would seem to be a better choice than a public relations person, usually it is not the job of the environmental official to prevent pollution at the plant. It is their job to measure the pollution once it is produced, keep track of it, and to try to control it. If you are talking to any of these three kinds of company representatives, you are not talking to someone with authority to make a decision.

These initial contacts can be valuable nevertheless. You can learn a lot about the company and how it operates, so always go with a battery of questions. They may have questions for you, too. You can raise repeatedly the need for direct talks with a decision-maker. In addition, you can get them to help you figure out which decision-maker is the best one to talk to.

It is not always obvious at the beginning who this is. It probably will not be anyone at a lower level than plant manager. Sometimes it will be someone at corporate headquarters.

As the campaign escalates, the company eventually realizes it is in their interest for a real decision-maker to talk with neighbors in earnest.

When it is in earnest—and you will be able to tell fairly soon—then the hard part of the campaign is over. They are ready to talk turkey. The rest may last for weeks or months, but if you do not let your concentration slip, it will produce a result you can be proud of.

At this point, you might consider finding someone who has been through these kinds of talks before. Ask them to be your free consultant for the duration of the talks. They do not have to live nearby. If they have a phone, they can be anywhere.

Introductory meeting

It often helps to meet the company's decision-maker one-on-one first.

You can introduce the executive to the unfamiliar process of working with his or her neighbors on a common problem. They will be more ready to meet with a larger group of neighbors once they understand who you are and what they are getting into. In other words, they are more scared than you are.

You should suggest that the meeting be one-on-one, but they might not take your suggestion. Sometimes they betray their fear by having a line-up of officials, for example, the president, the environmental vice president, a public relations officer and a lawyer. This military array faces one neighbor who arrives without an entourage, without even a notebook, just to talk with the president. If this happens to you, you are now part of a lasting image in all of their minds, with the caption, "What were we afraid of?"

If possible, meet on neutral ground, not in their office and not in your home. A coffee shop is a good choice. If they are too nervous to meet on neutral ground, it is not a big problem. In fact, it gives you a chance to show them you are not afraid to walk into their office by yourself.

There should not be a set script for such a meeting, but the following are the kinds of statements you can make that may help the executive adopt a constructive approach.

"We know you don't want to harm your neighbors."

"We want this campaign to be over as much as you do, and that's why we want to get down to work with you to solve our common problem."

"We don't view you as the problem. The pollution is the problem."

"We have a lot of interests in common, such as…"

"No one knows your operation better than you. That's why you need to be a partner in figuring out a solution."

"We're looking forward to the day when we can talk in the neighborhood and to the media about how the company is showing leadership in dealing with this."

"There have been a lot of campaigns like this in other places that have worked out well for both the company and the neighbors. I'd be glad to give you the names of some executives who can compare notes with you."

"In some campaigns, companies have made significant improvements at the plant, but didn't tell the neighbors. When you make changes, please tell us. We want to let people know the progress you're making."

You may find that the executive wants to vent a little at this meeting:

"You don't care about jobs."

"Are you a tool of the trial lawyers?"

"Are you ever going to be satisfied or are you going to complain forever?"

"I don't want to be a poster child for your fundraising."

"Your flyers are full of misstatements."

Let them vent. Getting this off their chests will leave them in a more constructive frame of mind. This is not a debate and no one is keeping score, so you do not have to worry about comebacks or responding to every comment. Show them by your example how to handle such a situation. There may be things they bring up that you can clarify or straighten out on the spot. If you notice an opportunity to say honestly, "Yes, you're right," don't miss it. Note differences without being belligerent. Even the tone of your voice can be a good example for them.

Some of the meeting should be spent discussing next steps, which will usually involve the details of a larger meeting: who, when, where, format and agenda.

It is probably a good idea to tell them that at the larger meeting, "It will end up more constructive if some of the neighbors first have a chance to tell you their stories. It may get a little heated. We are not interested in ambushing you or subjecting you to any kind of verbal abuse. That serves no purpose, and I won't let it happen. But it is important for people to be able to tell their stories. They've been waiting a long time. Let's figure out the best way to allow that."

Give the executive your phone number and email address if you have one, and tell them you want them to feel free to get in touch with you. "In a situation like this, it is better if there are no surprises. If you hear something, you can call me to ask about it, and vice versa. Is it easier if I call your secretary first? What's best for you?"

There is far more for you to talk about than you will have time for. Keep in mind that this first meeting is a success even if the only outcome is that each participant realizes that the other is a human being and not a cartoon character.

A larger meeting

Anne Rolfes, founding director of the Louisiana Bucket Brigade, gives her thoughts about who should go to the subsequent meetings and where it is best to have them:

> In every place, it's been from three community members to fifteen [going to meetings with the company], and the company has had from four up to ten or twelve people. Shell had the most people; they sent a lawyer for every person. And the lawyers never say anything.

The people who go to the meetings [with the company] are the people in the communities who have been the leaders and who have been present for things. It can get a little bit dicey when some people want to pull in somebody who hasn't been involved or who's been marginally involved and who they for some reason think would be really good. One of the criteria should be that it is someone who has been involved in the campaign for enough time to see what the company does and says and won't fall for something in negotiation and sell everybody out. It's a decision that the community makes and we have a conversation with them about it. It can be one of those difficult situations in which you may have different advice for people than they might want to hear. Advice such as that maybe they need to include some other people who've been involved, that other people do have opinions and its much more powerful if others are involved. 'You can't control this by yourself.'

Certainly, we do not want the meeting to be at the plant. We like it to be in the community. If it's at the plant, it's more intimidating to people. They feel less sure of themselves. I try to spend the most time before a meeting going through the campaign and archiving what they've done that's been powerful. I make the point about why this meeting is happening and that they are equals in this room. This person is not now handing down decisions; that's not how this works.

The biggest challenge, once the companies have agreed to meet, is to get the community to remember why the company is meeting in the first place: because they have demonstrated power. All of a sudden, people who have been powerful in nailing them, get a little bit nervous because they are going to meet with the head of this company.[2]

What happens next

The process can follow different paths.

---

2. Anne Rolfes (Founding Director, Louisiana Bucket Brigade), interview with author, Cleveland, Ohio, July 21, 2005.

This is all new to the company, and without your guidance, it will quickly fall back into its standard way of operating. For example, the company representatives may assume that one meeting is plenty, or that they and the neighbors should now meet quarterly to talk things through. Make sure they understand that this process is not to create a new committee, it is to solve a problem, and it should move forward on this project as fast as possible until it is completed. Maybe the full group doesn't need to meet again right away, but you and they need to decide now on the most productive process. There are many possibilities. For example, a smaller group can meet often to tackle different parts of the problem. If the problems are in two distinct areas, such as air and water pollution, two smaller working groups could be formed.

The company also needs help getting used to informal communication with its neighbors. Use the plant manager's number often. You don't need an emergency. You can call him or her two days after the meeting to see how they thought it went. Or say, "You know, there was something I meant to say at the meeting..." Or suggest another way of proceeding. Or mail them an article about how a similar company elsewhere solved a similar problem. It does not matter so much what it is about. It does matter that you break down the idea that the company and its neighbors can only communicate at awkward formal meetings. Sometimes the most productive meetings have been the most informal, one-on-one in a coffee shop, coming on short notice in the middle of a campaign.

Focus on the solution

You don't have to agree on everything.

It may seem like a good idea to try to come to agreement with the company step-by-step, starting with the problem and moving toward the solution. For example, you might propose the following set of statements to agree on: (1) The company is emitting this amount of such-and-such chemicals, (2) This creates hazardous levels of these chemicals in the neighborhood's air, (3) These levels are making people sick.

This approach may seem logical, but it will create a mess. The company representatives have spent years denying that their emissions could make people sick. To some extent, they actually believe the denials. Their law-yers are instructing them that any admission may be used against them in a lawsuit. If you insist on agreement on these points, it will slow down nego-tiations, and may derail them completely.

A better course is to realize that the company's presence at the table implies agreement with what you have been saying all along about the problem. You do not need to rub their faces in it. Both sides are there to find a solution, not to continue arguing about the problem.[3] Focus on the solution.

Accelerate the campaign

It is essential that the campaign accelerate during the negotiations. This shows that you know the campaign is the only reason why talks are being held. The stronger the campaign, the sooner a good outcome will emerge.

For the same reason, if the campaign goes into limbo once talks start, you can bet that the talks will also go into limbo before long. You have just taken the initiative from yourself.[4]

The company may regard the acceleration of the campaign as an unpleasant surprise and unfair as well. "We are negotiating in good faith, and it is only fair that you suspend your campaign against us." The answer is that we want to stop the campaign, too, but we can't until we have something to show for it. Of course, if the company would agree to sus-pend polluting the neighborhood during the talks, maybe something could be worked out.

No deals on the spot, and usually no deals at all

Sometimes people attending a meeting with a company decision-maker are worried that they may make a bad deal and let everyone down. Some-times neighbors who are not attending the meeting are wondering the same thing.

---

3. This does not, of course, rule out an agreement on principles, oral or written, at some point in the process, if both parties find it helpful.
4. For more on the role of initiative, see Chapter 4.

There is a way to keep these doubts from undermining your group's confidence and unity. You can decide that neighbors will not make any agreements at the same meeting where they are proposed. If the company makes a new proposal at a meeting, the neighbors' representatives tell them they will take it back to the community to discuss it before any decisions are made.

In practice, most good neighbor campaigns end with no formal agreement at all. Usually, the company suddenly issues a press release announcing its unilateral decision to invest a certain amount of money in modernizing the plant and thereby reducing emissions. The release acknowledges neither the neighbors nor the campaign.

This is the time to stop and think carefully about how the company's announcement measures up to the goals of your campaign. On the one hand, you need to make an assessment of whether and how people's daily lives will be improved if the company follows through. No victory is perfect; is this one good enough? On the other hand, to the degree it falls short of what you were seeking, what are your chances of a better outcome if you continue the campaign?

It is a tough call, especially if you or others have been in the conflict for five or ten years. You may feel that it is easier to do what is familiar, which is to keep fighting indefinitely, than to take the victory. Alternatively, you may be so hungry for something to call a victory, that you are tempted to lower your standards to declare a victory at the first sign of good news. Make sure your victory has to do with tangible improvements in neighbors' daily lives.

The important thing is to make a deliberate clear-headed decision.

A written agreement?

A unilateral company announcement is not the only way negotiations can end well. Sometimes, the parties end up signing a 'good neighbor agreement'.[5] Whether to propose a written agreement depends on the circumstances, of course. Such agreements may bring more clarity and specificity to the outcome, and the signatures on the bottom may convey more commitment than a press release would. They can, however, lead neighbors to think that the agreement is self-enforcing. It is not. The company can freely ignore a written agreement if it is confident that there will be no consequence for violating it.

The best way to help the company stick to an agreement, or a press release, is for the neighbors to stay alert and active.

Trust but verify

If you have decided that what the company says it will do, or has already done, seems to be enough, bring in an expert to look at the plans and the plant. Too much is at stake to rely on guesswork. Find the names of several experts from contacts you may already have, or ask state or national environmental resource groups. If there is a local union, maybe they can help. Once you have some names, see which of them the company would be willing to talk to about their plans. Usually a tour of the plant is needed, too.

The company usually bristles at this idea, but if you handle it well, they will come to see that it is a small price to pay for getting "this whole thing" behind them.

Ohio Citizen Action's Sandy Buchanan recalls, "To verify Brush Wellman's commitments for its Elmore plant, we proposed someone we knew was superb, occupational physician Dr. Kathy Fagan. For whatever reason, Brush Wellman balked. Fortunately, we had a second name, Peter Kowalski, an environmental health scientist at the federal Agency for Toxic Substances and Disease Registry.[6] We respected his judgment and he had already been inside the plant. Because both Brush and we accepted his report, the process moved forward."[7]

---

5. For more information on Good Neighbor Agreements, contact Sanford Lewis, Strategic Counsel on Corporate Accountability, P.O. Box 231, Amherst, MA 01004 (413) 549-7333, gnproject@earthlink.net, http://www.strategiccounsel.net, or Northern Plains Resource Council, 2401 Montana Avenue, Suite 200, Billings, Montana 59101, (406) 248-1154, info@northernplains.org, http://www.northernplains.org.

6. The Agency for Toxic Substances and Disease Registry (ATSDR), based in Atlanta, Georgia, is a federal public health agency of the U.S. Department of Health and Human Services.

Neighbors understandably can get frustrated about such obstacles, thinking that after everything that has happened, it could all be in jeopardy now. It does not have to be in jeopardy if you stay flexible and have back-up names.

Conversely, "If the company keeps pushing one person and you don't like him, you don't have to take it. You just problem-solve it with one another. Since you've problem-solved the rest of the campaign, it shouldn't be that hard," according to Rachael Belz of Ohio Citizen Action.[8]

Finally, do not forget to acknowledge publicly the progress the company is making. Yes, they hurt a lot of people. And they only settled under pressure and much too late. And it was shabby for them not to acknowledge you in their announcement. None of this matters now. This is the time to be generous with your words because you just won.

5. Follow-up

There are many ways to go about follow-up. The wrong way is to let them go, saying, 'OK, they are making the changes. Now we're done.'

Verifying their commitment leads directly to the follow-up stage since it establishes the first post-campaign relationships between the neighbors and the company. It also begins the development of trust between the parties.

To verify the original commitment, there is no substitute for an independent expert. Once trust develops during the follow-up stage, however, you can begin to rely on the company's word.

None of the progress in the follow-up stage is automatic, though. Sometimes, even if the company fulfills its original promises, the follow-up communications can remain rigid, contentious and distrustful. If so, it is a missed opportunity. Not only does trust head off trouble in the

---

7. Sandy Buchanan (Executive Director, Ohio Citizen Action) interview with author, Cleveland, Ohio, January 6, 2006.

8. Rachael Belz (Associate Director, Ohio Citizen Action) interview with author, Cincinnati, Ohio, January 6, 2006.

future, it can produce bigger health and safety improvements than did the original campaign victory. It depends on the people-skills on both sides.

In the Rohm and Haas campaign in Cincinnati, after the company made its commitment, the verifying phase took eight months of work by a company-neighbor working group. This creative "working group" approach was suggested by Syd Havely of Rohm and Haas' corporate home office in Philadelphia. He also suggested that a third party facilitator be involved for the duration of the working group. The working group was a success because it had the backing of the plant manager, Bruce Beiser, who made all of the on-site decisions; Rohm and Haas' corporate office; the neighbors and the environmental groups involved. Rohm and Haas was represented by Curt Lambert, an environmental engineer, who went out of his way to answer questions on the spot, and, according to Rachael Belz, "always found a way to explain to us what was happening and what they were thinking about, and to get input from us."[9] In this case, trust began to develop during the verifying stage. It came from people seeing the company following through with what they said they would do. Similarly, when Beiser came to the final meeting of the working group, he was surprised that the neighbors and working group members were so supportive of the plant. Belz said, "We'd gotten past the stage of talking about the problems, and were on to the concrete changes and timelines that were being proposed. It was obvious to everyone that the working group approach not only helped to iron out the specifics of the changes, but also gave us much needed time to build a new relationship between fenceline neighbors and plant officials."

Moving from the working group to the follow-up stage, Rohm and Haas proposed that the neighbors' group fold itself into its newly-formed Community Advisory Council. The neighbors agreed, on the condition that everyone involved would work together to make sure the Council had

9. Ibid.

the right representation and the structure included the four issues the campaign worked to resolve. Rachael Belz describes the Council meetings:

> The Council has been meeting ever since, nine times a year. At each meeting, the plant manager gives his plant update, followed by a discussion of sewer, air or water violations that have occurred. This is followed by the topic of the month, for example, emergency response. Much of the discussion is about the basics—goals, plans, and deadlines.
>
> Early on, you may not be sure whether the company is being straight with you. You will want to be able to check some of what they say. If, for example, they say they are going to install a new piece of equipment, they will have to get permits from the regulators. You can go to the regulatory agency yourself and ask them if they have received such an application from the company. If you keep finding that what the company says checks out, your trust in their word should start to build.
>
> One month, plant manager Bruce Beiser came to the monthly meeting and said that when they started to make some of the promised changes, they realized that almost all of their compressors dated back to the 1980s. The company had to replace all of them. If they had not done the project, they would not have figured that out and there could have been a serious break down.
>
> A couple of years ago, a new person in the group suggested that we didn't need to keep having nine meetings a year. I was shocked when the first person to speak up was Bruce Beiser. He said that he liked the meetings and appreciated the accountability. He said it was like balancing his checkbook. I couldn't believe it. The company feels good about coming and telling us whatever is going on, even when occasionally it is bad news. The Rohm and Haas campaign, especially the working group and the follow-up, was a model. It has been an incredible thing to see. The entire campaign, working group and community advisory council worked so well that Ohio Citizen Action gave a joint community-company "Good Neighbor Award" to six fenceline neighbors and the Rohm and Haas Cincinnati plant in December, 2004.

The continued good work of the working group was also highlighted. We were glad to give credit where credit was due.[10]

Having been persuaded to examine their operations, these companies often don't want to stop. They become ambitious to break new ground in both pollution prevention and health and safety. The follow-up is when the acceleration can happen.

10.Ibid.

▼

ENVIRONMENTAL HEALTH SYMPTOM SURVEY:

Concerned Citizens of New Sarpy, Louisiana, 2002

New Sarpy, on the Mississippi River 15 miles west of New Orleans, is home to 1,568 people and the massive Valero Energy St. Charles Refinery. In June 2002, neighbors used the following health symptom survey to learn more about what refinery pollution was doing to them.

These surveys, while informal and not 'scientific,' are excellent tools for uncovering patterns and alerting the community to potential problems. Denny Larson of Global Community Monitor recommends "tuning the survey" to pollutants and their acute or chronic health effects from target facility. Sample data can help with this. For example, if your plant emits large amounts of sulfur dioxide, ask on the survey about asthma attacks, which sulfur dioxide is known to trigger.

Do not put the respondent's name, address or any other identifying information on the survey. Under the wrong circumstances, the company might be able to subpoena the raw survey results in a lawsuit, and you do not want the neighbors' privacy threatened that way.

For more on health surveys, consult "Community Health Surveys," from the Center for Health Environment and Justice, P.O. Box 6806, Falls Church, VA 22043, (703) 237-2249, http://chej.org.—Ed.

SURVEY GOALS

- To begin to build a body of information about the general health status of our community.

- To raise the question in every household in our community of the possibility of a link between environmental pollution and personal health.

- To serve as an additional step in the evaluation of health problems in our community.

- To develop information about the health status of our residents that will be of interest to the medical community.

- To help in the effort of identifying problems that can be corrected.

CRITERIA FOR INTERVIEWERS

With the current estimate of 130 households for the symptom survey, a group of 13 interviewers would need to cover 10 houses each. Assuming four individuals to each household, each interviewer would conduct up to 40 interviews. According to the current schedule, the interviews would take place from July 7 to 13, 2002.

Interviewers must be able to—

- Physically reach the interviewees. Interviewers will have to walk and/or drive from house to house and walk through houses and up and down steps as needed.

- Work as necessary to complete the survey. Assuming all goes well, interviewers will have to put in approximately 6 hours and 40 minutes actually performing interviews, at 10 minutes per interview. This does not include time to get from house to house, nor does it include extra time between interviews. All interviews would need to be performed during the week of July 7-13, 2002.

- Follow directions. It is absolutely necessary that interviewers follow directions exactly as they are given during training and on the Survey form itself. This will help to ensure that the information that each interviewer collects is consistent.

- Speak clearly and communicate well. Interviewers must be able to speak clearly and be understood by the people whom they are interviewing. Interviewers should treat interviewees with respect and kindness at all times.

- Record responses of the interviewees without bias. Interviewers must record exactly what the interviewees say, without interpreting or changing their answers. Interviewers must not, in any way attempt to influence the way in which the interviewees answer the questions. Interviewees must not allow their personal feelings or opinions affect the way in which they record responses.

- Be knowledgeable. Interviewers should be knowledgeable about the goals and timeline of the symptom survey and about the activities and meeting times of the Concerned Citizens of New Sarpy organization. Interviewers should answer any questions that interviewees have about the survey or the Concerned Citizens of New Sarpy and, if they do not know the answer to a question, they should direct the question to someone who does.

SURVEY QUESTIONNAIRE

Hello. My name is_____.I am doing a survey of community health conditions for the Concerned Citizens of New Sarpy. I would like to ask you a few questions about your health. It should only take about ten minutes of your time. This is a voluntary survey, and you may refuse to answer any or all of the questions without fear of any consequences. May I begin?

[If "NO."] Thank you for your time. Have a nice day.

[If "YES."] Thank you. Neither your name, nor your address or phone number will be written on this survey. Therefore, no one will know how you answer the survey questions. Let me remind you that this survey is entirely voluntary. You may refuse to answer any of the questions, and you may ask me to stop at any time.

[Begin Survey form.]

Survey form
ID Code:_____

1. Number of persons in the house_____

2. Age of subject_____

3. Sex_____

[If subject is 17 years old or younger, another person in the household should answer the questions.]

4. Relationship of person answering questions to subject
_____

5. Do you live in New Sarpy for most of the year?
□ YES   □ NO   □ Did not answer

6. How many years have you lived in this house?

_____ □ Did not answer

7. How many years have you lived in New Sarpy?

_____ □ Did not answer

8a. Do you cough on most days of the week?

□ YES □ NO □ Did not answer

8b. *[If "YES."]* How many years have you had the cough?

_____ □ Did not answer

9a. Do you bring up mucus on most days of the week?

□ YES □ NO □ Did not answer

9b. *[If "YES."]* How many years have you had this problem?

_____ □ Did not answer

10. When you breathe, do you sound wheezy or like you are whistling?

□ YES □ NO □ Did not answer

11. Have you ever gone to the emergency room because you were wheezing or because you were having a hard time breathing?

□ YES □ NO □ Did not answer

12. Do you walk more slowly than other people your age because you wheeze or lose your breath?

□ YES □ NO □ Did not answer

13. Has a doctor or nurse ever told you that you have asthma?

□ YES □ NO □ Did not answer

14. Has a doctor or nurse ever told you that you have chronic bronchitis?

□ YES □ NO □ Did not answer

15. Do you have frequent or severe headaches, including migraines?
□ YES □ NO □ Did not answer

16. Do your eyes often water or itch when you go outside?
□ YES □ NO □ Did not answer

17. Do you feel tired more often than not?
□ YES □ NO □ Did not answer

18. While living in New Sarpy, have you ever had two weeks or more during which you felt sad, blue, depressed, or when you lost all interest and pleasure in things that you usually cared about?
□ YES □ NO □ Did not answer

19. Do you have trouble using your hands to do simple things?
□ YES □ NO □ Did not answer

20a. Have you ever had cancer?
□ YES □ NO □ Did not answer

20b. *[If "YES."]* What kind of cancer?
_____ □ Did not answer

21. What other health problems do you have?
_____

_____

□ Did not answer

WOMEN ONLY

22a. Have you ever had a miscarriage?
☐ YES ☐ NO ☐ Did not answer

22b. *[If "YES."]* **How many miscarriages have you had?**
_____ ☐ Did not answer

22c. If you can remember, what was/were the date(s) of the miscarriage(s)?
_____

23. How many times have you been pregnant altogether?
_____ ☐ Did not answer

24. Do you have health problems that you think may be caused by the air in your neighborhood?
☐ YES ☐ NO ☐ Did not answer

25. Do you often feel anxious or nervous about living near an oil refinery?
☐ YES ☐ NO ☐ Did not answer

[When you have completed the survey form, make sure that you have marked an answer for every question, and give the interviewee a Health Survey Contact Card.]

Thank you for being a part of our health survey. Here are the phone numbers of the survey coordinators in case you have any questions or comments about the survey. Please feel free to contact them at any time. Also on the card is the phone number of the Tulane University Institutional Review Board, which has reviewed this project for the purposes of protecting human subjects. You may call them as well with any questions or complaints.

Now I will put your answers to the survey questions away. The Concerned Citizens of New Sarpy would like you to have a copy of any report that comes out of this survey. We would also like to invite you to our next meeting on August_____.

A. Would you like to receive a copy of any report based on this survey?
[If "YES," write the person's name, address and phone number on Contact List.*]*

B. Would you be interested in going to a meeting with your neighbors to talk about health and the environment in your community?
[If "YES," write the person's name, address and phone number on Contact List.*]*

C. If anyone living in this household died of cancer within the last 10 years, would you like to have his or her name included in a special memorial to victims of cancer from New Sarpy?
☐ YES ☐ NO ☐ Did not answer
[If "YES," write the person's name, address and phone number on Contact List.*]*

Is there another person who lives in your household through most of the year that I may speak with at this time?

[If "NO."] Thank you again for your time. Have a nice day!
[If "YES," and the person is 17 years old or younger.] Due to this person's youth, can you answer the survey questions about him/her?
[If "YES," and the person is 18 years old or older.] Thank you again for your time.
[Begin a new survey form with this next person.]

APPENDIX B

▼

THE THINGS YOU DON'T KNOW

In 2003, Universal Purifying Technology, a California company, wanted to turn the former Columbus trash-burning power plant into a giant facility to melt tires. The company would wash and dry scrap tires, shred tire chips, and melt tires into scrap steel, synthesis gas, oils, and carbon black. The plant would process 8,333 pounds of tires an hour, 24 hours a day. Southside neighbors launched an aggressive campaign to stop this project, one of the highlights of which was Teresa Mills' devastating testimony reproduced here. This is a model for how to mix a little homework with a lot of common sense.

The neighbors won, and the tire-melting scheme was abandoned.—Ed.

Testimony
Teresa Mills, Director
Buckeye Environmental Network

November 6, 2003
Ohio EPA public hearing
Columbus, Ohio

My name is Teresa Mills; I am the director of the Buckeye Environmental Network, and a member of the Southwest Neighbors Protecting Our Environment. Our address is P.O. Box 182, Grove City 43123. My comments are made on behalf of the Buckeye Environmental Network, Southwest Neighbors Protecting Our Environment and the citizens of Franklin County. We offer comments here tonight and reserve the right to make further comment up until the close of the comment period.

One of the values instilled in me by my parents was that "People don't care how much you know, until they know how much you care." Right now, I care more about the things you don't know when it comes to this process. Let me list just some of the things you don't know.

1. You do not know how the tire chips will be fed into the reactor.

2. You do not know how the auger moves the tires in the six pass process within the reactor.

3. You do not know the height of the reactor even though the height of the reactor and the process structure is listed in the application as a process hazard.

4. You do not know how long the reactor will be.

5. You do not know the residence time within the reactor.

6. You do not know the amount of fugitive emissions from the reactor even though every non-welded connection to this reactor is a possible point of leakage. This includes the inlet and outlet connection, the points where the auger shafts penetrate the reactor, and any points where instruments penetrate the reactor.

7. You do not know why there is a sampling valve in the reactor.

8. You do not know where the pressure relief valve on the reactor will be located.

9. You do not know how often this pressure relief valve will be used.

10. You will not know when this pressure relief valve releases uncontrolled pollution into our air, because you do not require any monitoring or reporting of this valve. You also do not require that the emission from this valve be routed to a pollution control device.

11. You do not know how Universal Purifying Technology will guarantee that the reactor will operate in a vacuum.

12. You do not know if there will be excess oxygen within the reactor.

13. You do not know the temp. range within the reactor.

14. You do not know how Universal Purifying Technology will prevent the typical problems associated with screw type reactors, such as material backup due to the metals in the chips.

15. You do not know how the melted material will exit the reactor.

16. You do not know when or how often the pressure relief valve in the filter will be used.

17. You do not know when or how often the pressure relief valve in condenser # 1 or #2 will be used.

18. You do not know what the catalyst used inside the reactor will be.

19. You do not know the chemical composition of the catalyst and how it will effect emissions.

20. You do not know how the catalyst will be stored on site.

21. You do not know how much of the catalyst will be stored.

22. You do not know how or if the air lock down stream from the cooling unit will work to prevent air from catching the melted material on fire.

23. You do not know how the company will assure that air does not enter the conveyor containing the carbon black dust, which could cause an explosion.

24. You do not know what steps Universal Purifying Technology will take if there is an emergency condition that would necessitate the shut down of the facility, such as an explosion or fire.

25. You do not know where the company will obtain the necessary pollution control equipment. They could in all reality purchase used control equipment.

26. You do not know the temperature range and retention time within the wet scrubber.

27. You do not know if by trying to drop the temperature of the gas exiting the incinerator it will be quick enough to stop the formation of dioxin.

28. You do not know if dioxin will form in the carbon activation furnaces.

I could go on but I think you get my point. No reasonable person could have concluded that there was a basis for the agency claim that no or little dioxin would be formed due to these critical gaps in information.

I understand that Ohio EPA considers this source a minor source of air pollution and the citizens a major inconvenience in this process that has a pre-determined outcome, but: How on God's green earth did you issue the draft permit for this facility?

Anti-glossary

The problems we work on are all political, not in the sense of candidates and elections, but rather "Who's making these decisions?" In every campaign, there are the people who have been making the decisions and the people who have had to live with the consequences. They are different groups. Had they been the same, these problems would not exist, and we would be living in a democracy.

Every campaign is about the neighbors pushing their way into the decision-making, and the polluter and the government trying to keep them out.

One of the ways they try to keep people out is to speak a language no one can understand. They want people to be intimidated and bewildered and say, "I'm just not qualified to make this decision. I can't even figure out what they are talking about."

For example, there is a federal garbage law. It is easy for anyone to figure out what "federal garbage law" means. That is why no corporate or government bureaucrat will describe it that way.

First, they call it "solid waste" rather than "garbage." This is supposed to distinguish it from "hazardous waste," but hazardous waste can come in solid form and garbage has plenty of hazardous waste in it. This is not confusing enough, however, so they refer to it by the name of the law, the "Resource Conservation and Recovery Act." That's a twelve-syllable mouthful, so then they shorten it to the acronym, "RCRA." Of course, "RCRA" still has four syllables, so they say "Rek-ra." Now it sounds like an ancient Egyptian god. They've created a verbal garbage dump, with "Rek-ra" lying on top of it. Only by digging down through the muck can you find out what they are talking about.

The company and the government talk like this for a specific purpose. It is not general perversity; it's to keep us out.

There are many words and phrases designed to confuse. Here are a few to avoid:

> *adverse impact:* harm
> *adversely impacts human health:* makes people sick
> *beneficial impact:* help
> *brownfield:* abandoned factory site
> *carcinogenic:* cancer-causing
> *economically disadvantaged:* poor
> *emission event:* see *malfunction*
> *endocrine:* hormone
> *environmental justice community:* community experiencing environmental *in*justice, namely that chemical plants settle in poor neighborhoods, many of which are populated primarily by African-Americans, Hispanics and other minorities
> *health effect:* illness or injury
> *incident:* see *malfunction*
> *malfunction:* fireball, inferno, blaze, spewing, disgorging, pouring forth, eruption, spitting up, spitting out, expulsion, dumping, purging, belching, heaving
> *morbidity:* sickness
> *mortality:* death
> *off-site:* into the neighborhood
> *particulates:* soot
> *regulated community:* polluters
> *solid waste:* garbage
> *take a hard look at:* do nothing
> *Title V:* air pollution permit
> *upset:* see malfunction

Acronyms are another favorite way to cut people out of the discussion. There are a few well-known acronyms, like "U.S.," "EPA" and "FBI." Beyond those, industry and bureaucrats have created thousands of obscure in-crowd acronyms, like "HMS" (highway mobile source), "NAA" (non-attainment area), and "BACT" (best available control technology).

Those using this baffling language want neighbors to think they will also be baffled by the advanced ideas being discussed. This is just so much applesauce, however: the most important ideas about pollution are understandable by anyone over the age of eight. For example, "You made the mess, you clean it up," or "What you don't have can't leak."[1]

When we insist that everyone speak plain English, then everyone can have a say.

---

1. Trevor Kletz, *What Went Wrong? Case Studies of Process Plant Disasters* (Burlington, MA: Gulf Professional Publishing, 1998), 369.

Contributors

Rachael Belz is the Executive Director of the Ohio Citizen Action Education Fund. She was Ohio Citizen Action's Southwest Ohio Program Director from 1996–2003, where she directed winning good neighbor campaigns with Cincinnati Specialties, Rohm and Haas Cincinnati, AK Steel in Middletown and the Sunoco Toledo Refinery.

Sandy Buchanan is executive director of Ohio Citizen Action, the state's largest environmental organization. Buchanan began work with the organization as a student intern in 1977, after graduating from Cornell University. She has directed successful statewide campaigns for toxic chemical right-to-know laws, and helped craft the federal right-to-know law enacted in 1986. She has worked with community organizations across Ohio to win pollution prevention campaigns, and serves as a board member for the Environmental Working Group. Buchanan and her husband, Bill Whitney, live in Cleveland with their two sons.

Hilton Kelley is Executive Director of Community In-power and Development Association in Port Arthur, Texas; Chair of the National Bucket Brigade Coalition; and Field Coordinator of the National Refinery Reform Campaign. In a 2004 lawsuit settlement, his Port Arthur organization acquired two real-time toxic air monitors that can detect more than 300 volatile organic and industrial compounds. Kelley has traveled all over the United States with these monitors, helping other fenceline neighbor groups learn what they are breathing.

Kim Klein is internationally known as a fundraising trainer, consultant and author. She is best known for adapting traditional fundraising techniques, particularly major donor campaigns, to the needs of organizations with small budgets working for social justice. She is the Chardon Press Series Editor at Jossey-Bass Publishers, which publishes and distributes materials that help to build a stronger nonprofit sector, and the founder and publisher of the *Grassroots Fundraising Journal*. Widely in demand as a speaker, Kim Klein has provided training and consultation in all 50 states and in 20 countries. She is an adjunct faculty member at the Haas School of Business, University of California Berkeley.

Denny Larson is the Director of the Global Community Monitor, www.gcmonitor.org, an international human rights and environmental justice organization. Denny has 21 years of experience working with industrial communities as an organizer, technical advisor and communications specialist. He began his education about refinery neighbors and their plight as a door-to-door canvasser in 1984 in the San Francisco Bay area's "cancer belt" of Contra Costa County. In 1994, Larson organized the nation's first national network of oil refinery neighbors, workers and shareholders. In 1995, he developed the "Bucket Brigade" method of air sampling and environmental monitoring for industrial neighbors. Since then, he has continued his work of helping communities start "Bucket Brigades" and other empowerment strategies in order to win environmental justice around the globe. Bucket Brigades are now active in 12 countries and dozens of communities in the United States.

Teresa Mills turned from a housewife to an activist in 1994 as she led her neighborhood to victory over the Columbus, Ohio, trash-burning power plant. She has gone on to become nationally-recognized as one of the most reliable resources on toxic pollution and neighborhood organizing. Teresa Mills is the director of the Buckeye Environmental Network, which offers guidance and technical assistance to citizen groups facing toxic hazards. In 2003, she received the Howard M. Metzenbaum Ohio Citizen Action Award, the organization's highest honor.

John O'Connor (1954–2001) was an organizer, author, and environmental entrepreneur. After graduating from Clark University, he became an organizer in a low-income Worcester neighborhood, and helped build the Massachusetts Fair Share organization. O'Connor founded the National Toxics Campaign in 1983 and was a leader in the fight to pass the federal Superfund clean-up law. He co-edited the book *Fighting Toxics* (1990), and co-authored two other books, *Who Owns the Sun?* (1997) and *Getting the Lead Out* (2001). O'Connor founded Greenworks, a corporation to help finance environmental start-up companies, the Irish Famine Memorial Committee, and the Health Action Alliance.

Paul Ryder is the Organizing Director for Ohio Citizen Action. He has worked for Ohio Citizen Action in Cleveland since 1977, except for a six-year leave as policy director for Ohio Governor Richard Celeste. Before coming to Ohio, he worked as national staff for the Indochina Peace Campaign in Santa Monica, and researcher for the Ellsberg-Russo Legal Defense in the Pentagon Papers Trial in Los Angeles.

Index

978-0-595-38651-2
0-595-38651-2

2100776

Made in the USA